sales
tales

The Hustle, Humor, and
Lessons from a Life in Sales

sales
tales

MANDI GRAZIANO

MERACK

www.mandigraziano.com

Published and distributed by Merack Publishing.

Library of Congress Control Number: 2021914740
Graziano, Mandi
Sales Tales: The Hustle, Humor, and Lessons from a Life in Sales
ISBN Paperback 978-1-949635-94-2
ISBN Hardcover 978-1-949635-96-6
ISBN eBook 978-1-949635-95-9

dedication

Mama K and Grandpa Jim: because your
creative spirit and energy gave me that
burning fire in my belly to write.

Kimmy: because I told you I would when we
were at Turf Club back in 2009.

Scooter My Love: because of your support in
all my endeavors. I love you.

contents

introduction

Sales is not a dirty word. I used to think it was, so I lied about my first sales job. (I said I was a consultant—which I was—but it was all sales, all the time.) The stigma from sales needs to be removed. Everyone needs sales. Salespeople are not liars. Salespeople are not schmucks. Salespeople are not bullshitters. It bums me out when people say these things because they are saying it about me—a career salesperson.

A good salesperson is an educator, a listener, a problem solver and yes, a consultant. This is the reason I wrote this book. I want people to stop cringing when they hear the word sales. Whether you know it or not, you too have many sales moments in your life. I want to help people embrace these moments as an opportunity to get something better for themselves. I wrote this book in a funny, relatable way to disarm the sales process and help you understand it better so you can be more accepting of the concept of sales in your life. Having sales skills will make you better in the world and in the workforce.

Hopefully this book will help to illuminate your own sales moments so you can appreciate them.

This book is for salespeople and businesspeople. This book is also for that parent of four that needs to persuade the kids to get up, eat breakfast, and be out of the house by eight am every day. This book is for the engineer with an innovative idea and brilliant technical skills, but needs to learn how to pitch to investors. This book is for the entrepreneur who does not have a boss or director of sales hounding her for numbers and forecasts—yet needs some fresh ideas and accountability to grow her business. This book is for all of us. We need sales in our life. We need to learn how to sell earlier than in our twenties and thirties. It surprises me that some of the smartest people I know who have an MBA often shy away from sales tasks, whether it's negotiation, finding new customers or asking for business. This is because we do not teach deep levels of sales at an early age. Most people get their sales pedigree "on the job" and become quasi experts by age forty or fifty. Whether you are in business, a teacher, a doctor, or a pet groomer—you need sales. We need to be teaching our kids sales along with math and science in elementary school, and sharing deeper concepts of it as they progress through school. We use sales in every aspect of our lives. Learning this earlier in life benefits us all.

Sales Tales is a passionately-told collection of stories that spans the past twenty-five years of my business life. These are stories from bosses I've had, business people I've coached, co-workers and friends I adore, and my personal stories of sales interactions as a customer, buyer, sales leader and coach across the globe. Throughout the book I will introduce you to many of these people. We will hear their tales and they will share their experience working with me as a coach, client, vendor, salesperson or friend. This book is mostly entertaining, but I bet you find a nugget or two you can apply to your daily life. Although the book is written in the order of a typical sale (prospecting, networking, building relationships, making a presentation, closing business, firing clients and running a business through a crisis), you don't have to read the book in order. You can pick up whichever chapter strikes your fancy and tackle it as you wish. Sit back, relax and enjoy the melody. These are my Sales Tales.

Mandi Graziano

CHAPTER ONE

keep your antennae up

There is business everywhere, you just have to pay attention to the world around you, look up and look for it. - Mandi-ism

Finding new business can be daunting. Where do you begin? Who do you talk to? What do you talk about? I believe there are several approaches to finding business: Eavesdropping, Prospecting, Being Nice To Your Neighbors, Reading, Sharing Your Story with Friends and Family, and Keeping Your Antennae Up are just some of them.

sales tale:

MY VERY FIRST SALES MENTOR WAS A STRIPPER

I met my first mentor when I was just out of high school. I was working at a fitness center in Ohio as a personal trainer, gym membership salesperson, and an aerobics instructor. My mentor was my boss and I adored her. She had been in the fitness business for many years and her body was ripped. She had golden blonde hair with deep blue eyes & looked like She-Ra the Princess of Power, from the He-Man series. She was tough as nails and sharp as a tack, but was sweet as peach pie to me. I learned so much from her, starting with how to make a prospecting call. She schooled me on opening up the white pages, calling housewives in the area, asking them what they are doing for themselves, and convincing them to come in and take a tour of the all-women's fitness center in their neighborhood. Women would come in, tired, haggard—often with baby spit-up on their shirts. After arriving they'd put their kids in the childcare room and we'd give them an awesome workout. It was one small part of the day that each individual woman had dedicated to herself. Sometimes it was a couple of hours, other times it was just twenty minutes. They left sweaty, renewed, and smiling. They came back for classes and workouts and all the women networked with each other in the gym. Conversations about carpools, pickups, and sleep were had over a treadmill and step machine. I was proud of the work we did at our "all-ladies" fitness center because women's bodies, minds, and lives were really changing. I bought in completely to the lifestyle.

My boss would sit next to me with each prospecting call I made and tell me what I did well and what I could do better on the next one. (I would carry this tactic on in my own sales coaching business as I was teaching new salespeople to make prospecting calls—or reviving a seasoned salesperson's drive to sell.) When I got bored of cold calling people, we would hit the streets. She and I would walk into nearby businesses with the intention of making friends and spreading awareness about our new gym in the neighborhood. She would softly explain that we are their new neighbors and asked if they had heard of us. Most said no. She would explain who we were and what we did and then she would invite them in to try one of our classes or come by for a free workout. Her approach was very casual—she was your gal pal, BFF style. It was disarming and anyone that met her wanted to be her friend within seconds. She was so damn smart and super funny. She smiled. She asked questions. She listened. She used the person's name when speaking to them. She was sincere in her approach and she really made friends with each merchant neighbor.

Just before we would leave each business she would say, "By the way, would you mind helping us out by putting this box in your lobby so your customers can try us out for free too?" At that point, the business owner was so endeared to her, they always said yes. She would say, "Hold on, the box is in my car, let me go get it." That would be my signal to go out, get the box and sign-up forms, and bring it in. She would then offer to take coupons or brochures from their business and put them in our lobby.

I liked the approach of not hauling everything into the cold call because that would often cause concern to the person we were meeting. Instead, we would go get the box after we established rapport and felt it was appropriate. I would clear those boxes for signups once a week and these were now leads for my cold calls. I worked those lead forms like nobody's business and my boss would coach me with each call. She would say, "Next time wait for them to answer your questions," or, "Talk slower." Sometimes it was, "Smile when you talk so people can feel your energy," or, "Be sure to ask for the appointment before you hang up." I was a good soldier and did everything she said. She nicknamed me "Little Fox." I am not sure why she picked that name, but I took it as a term of endearment. I felt like I was in a school of sales.

All of her sales lessons were working. Women were coming in by the dozens. We were so busy doing tours, booking memberships, and filling the club that we had to hire more "Little Foxes." I had been attending community college and was saving for my first year of "away" college. Making commissions on the new memberships and hitting my sales goals was really helping with my savings.

Eventually, I was managing the club, working more and more hours, and opening up the place. My boss started coming in later and later in the day, and sometimes she would even take naps in the childcare room when no kids were in there. It was very strange, but I just thought she was tired and that's what real grownups did. This was my first "real job" that wasn't an ice cream shop or a catering company, so I didn't know what was normal at the time. I remember one time she brought in a box of colorful underwear thongs wrapped in cellophane. I had never seen underwear like that in my life. It was lacey, silky and beautiful. She opened the box and threw a pair in the wrapper at me as if she were playing a game of "think fast."

I caught it, opened it and looked at it. I held it up but was afraid to touch it, even though it was wrapped and unused. I unwrapped it and rubbed it on my arm to test it. It felt so soft and silky. I couldn't imagine this string being up my ass. It looked extremely uncomfortable. Many years later I would find the value in a good thong and the prevention of panty lines, but at that time, I was mystified as to why someone would want to wear these teeny tiny little things.

I asked her, "Why do you have these?"

She said, "Oh Little Fox, I am not making as much money as I need to survive so I dance at night."

"Where do you dance?" I asked. She told me the name of a popular place near the airport that we all knew to be a strip club. She said that is why she had been so tired. She really seemed to like the dancing gig and having more money seemed to stress her out less. It seemed like a difficult life, working two jobs. Both were physically strenuous, and both took up so much time. It made me feel sad for her that she didn't have much time left for herself other than a couple measly hours of sleep. It also made me mad at the owners for creating the payment structure in a way that caused my mentor to have to work two jobs. Ultimately, these were all her choices, and it sat deep with me for many years. I never wanted to get into a position where I had to take a second job just to pay the bills. I also wanted to be a part of the writing of the incentive plan, if possible, so I could be an effective leader and not worry about paying my bills in the future. She was such a talented salesperson and I feel the payment structure took away from her ability to be everything she could be in that role. What I didn't know then—but so clearly understand now—is that I was making more money than my boss. As a salesperson, I was paid an hourly rate, overtime and commission. My boss was paid a salary plus benefits but her commission structure was low. She was not incentivized from each sale like I was. She was incentivized based partially on team sales and other profit markers and a matrix that, overall, seemed unattainable. It's common in many sales structures for the boss or director to make less than the salespeople, because the higher you get up the chain, the more complicated the commission structure can get. I would carry this lesson with me for many years, and when I had the opportunity to make a change to sales salary structures, commissions, and deployments, I did.

Later that summer, after gym sales died down, I left for "away" college. I do not know what happened to my boss—or the fitness center for that matter—but I have such fond memories of that place and learned many valuable lessons.

THE LESSONS:

1. There is immense value in knowing the neighbors of your business.

2. Reciprocity with counterpart businesses is important.

3. Don't be afraid to pick up the phone and call a stranger, because you might be giving them a new lease on life with the product you are selling.

4. Ask open-ended questions to uncover a need and solve customer problems.

5. Most importantly, I learned that some day when I became the boss, I needed to ask for enough money so that I could pay my bills and not have to take a second job at a strip club—or anywhere else other than my main gig.

sales tale:

WATCHING REALITY TELEVISION CAN LEAD TO NEW CLIENTS

People always ask me, "Mandi, how do you find new business or clients?" I tell them, "Business is everywhere, you just have to look up." I really believe this. If you keep your antennae up, business is all around you. Literally look up, eavesdrop, listen to conversations, read magazines, look for clues—get your head out of your stinkin' phone, and observe your surroundings. For example, I was watching Millionaire Matchmaker many years ago. Patti Stanger was a matchmaker for millionaires. She vetted candidates for the millionaires to ensure the dating prospects were not gold diggers, and she set them up with potential wife/husband material. The show was pure gold— and it ended up being pure gold for my wallet too. While watching the show, I noticed the girl Patti was vetting was a meeting planner for an aerospace company in Orange County. I googled, "first name Meeting Planner Aerospace Company Orange County" and VOILA, there she was. I called the main line and asked to be connected to the girl. I got her voicemail. As I was transferred around, I paid attention to the last four digits of the line they were transferring me to, and tried the main line plus the last four digits and found her direct line. I called this girl for two months. I never left a message. I called at different times of the day. Finally, on the thirteenth call, she answered.

Immediately the tone of her voice was tentative, as if she regretted picking up her phone line. This is a standard tone I was used to hearing when I prospected for new business. The tone fueled me, it never scared me. I had a personal goal of turning that frown upside down—just like Lionel Kiddie City wanted me too. Here's how the conversation went.

Millionaire Matchmaker Candidate Potential New Customer (M.M.C.P.N.C.): "Hello" (annoyed voice)

Me: "So, I have to know what happened on the date, was he annoying or was it awesome?"

M.M.C.P.N.C.: "What? Who is This?"

Me: "Mandi Kobasic (my maiden name) with HPN Global. I am calling about your meetings, but am more interested in hearing how that Millionaire Matchmaker date went."

A PAUSE. THIS COULD GO ANYWHERE—
AND IT WAS A RISK.

M.M.C.P.N.C.: "It was awful, the guy was a jerk. Why are you calling me again?"

Me: "Oh, sorry the date sucked. The guy did seem like a jerk. Anyway, I find hotels all over the world for your meetings. I have been calling you for two months. I saw that you were a meeting planner on the show and thought I could help."

M.M.C.P.N.C.: "Honestly, you're the first person that has tracked me down from that show for a business reason. Most of the calls or mail that I've received have been from perverts or weirdos. What can you do for my meetings?"

I proceeded to ask her about what she does for her meetings, and how she sources and finds hotels. We interjected every now and again with snippets from the show. I was obsessed with Patti and wanted to know more about her and the process overall. By the time we hung up, I had secured two new meetings. Even though this person is not with the company anymore, I still have that company as an account.

THE LESSONS:

1. Be persistent.
2. Make the calls or emails. Don't stop at one. Keep going.
3. Pay attention when you're watching TV, there could be leads there for you.

andy's tale:

Andy is and was one of the best salespeople and humans I know. We worked together for two different companies over the years. He is an assertive and eager cold caller and creatively finds ways to engage with prospects. I've heard him on calls where he instantly befriends the prospect. He would say things like, "You have to give this a shot, you have to try this out." He really meant it. He really believed in the service or product he was selling and that came through to the other end of the phone. His demeanor is that of a really smart buddy. He knows his numbers and is prepared whenever he engages with a potential customer. He's always been hungry to look for business—like a pirate seeking out a hidden treasure. We belonged to a sales strategy team together called the West Coast Posse. Andy was so diligent about the many ways of finding new business and made the process fun and invigorating. He used to send me emails and within seconds I would feel his presence standing behind me. He'd then say, "Did you get my email?" He was so excited about finding new business, he wanted to talk about it the minute he found some. Having him on the team helped me dive deep into the strategy of total account management. He was a natural at this tactic. Each person on the West Coast Posse sold something different, however, when one person identified a potential prospect, it was up to that salesperson to uncover all the needs from that one client at one time. That meant that the client was only dealing with one person for all his/her business needs, instead of many different salespeople at one company. Andy was and is still a strategic master at cross selling and having fun in the sales process.

"Mandi is the first person I met who made prospecting fun. Mandi introduced me to the "total team sell" approach to prospecting. Prior to this, most prospecting made me, as the seller, feel cold, isolated, and rejected. From team-based activities to targeted outbound efforts, Mandi forever changed my perspective on cold calling. "

Andy Hottenstein, Regional Director, Business Development at Compass-USA

sales tale:
EAVESDROPPING IS GOOD
FOR BUSINESS

Back in the early 2000s, I worked with a smart colleague who taught me something interesting about hair salons. He went to a super fancy hair salon to get his hair cut once a month. I did not understand why he needed to go so frequently. As we neared the opening of our swanky private event venue, the frequency of his hair salon visits increased, now going every other week. When I asked him why he was going to such a fancy hair salon so often, he shared that it was a marketing tactic. He said the staff and the customers at that hair salon were the perfect demographic and a great customer for the new venue. I was floored. **This dude had a haircut strategy that had nothing to do with beauty and everything to do with business.** I thought about the number of times I'd been to a hair salon and eavesdropped on the conversation next to or behind me. I do it all the time, not just at the hair salon. Many good leads can come from eavesdropping. In this case, the salon was a couple blocks from the venue. If the guests and the staff heard about a great new location opening steps away from their work or salon, why wouldn't they go in and check it out? He was excited about the venue, and he got the other hair salon patrons excited about the venue as well. I am sure after he left, there were whispers of curiosity about the venue. If you have something to share, a hair salon may be a great place for it. Think about the places in your community that emulate the hair salon experience and replicate this model. Is it your favorite coffee shop? Tire rotation place? Doctor's office? Take a seat, talk to your peers, and listen. You may learn a hot tip or trend that benefits your business, and in turn, they may learn that your business is great for them.

sales tale:
A DELAYED FLIGHT MIGHT MEAN A NEW CLIENT

One of my gal pals famously tells a story about how she found a customer in an airport security line. Her flight had been delayed. She said to herself, "This is happening for a reason and I am going to find a client." Sure enough, as she traversed the security line, she ran into an old customer. They had lost touch and he had not realized she was still in the industry. Their gates were near each other and they happened upon the same hotel bar. Right there, while they sipped their tequila on the rocks with five limes, an unintended sales call happened. She was so determined to get a new customer that she bought him another round and explained what she was up to and how she could help. With a little buzz, and the sweet smell of victory, my gal pal headed to her flight with a new customer and new lead for when she returned to work. This is a great example of looking at life in a positive way. A lesser businessperson might have looked at that delay as a problem, something to complain about, and texted her family and friends about the delay. Instead, she used her time wisely, put her antennas up and found an old friend in the security line. If her head was stuffed in her phone, complaining, or if she did not silently chant to herself, "I'm going to find a customer," then she might have one less client.

This exercise of keeping your antenna up and paying attention to your surroundings reminds me of one of my favorite writers, David Sedaris. He famously takes a stroll for a couple hours every day in his neighborhood picking up trash. He leaves his phone at home and just pays attention to his surroundings. Some of his neighbors think he is homeless, some think he works for the city as a street cleaner, and some just completely ignore him. What he is doing is looking for stories and writing material. He believes that by paying attention to your surroundings, and putting your phone down for a couple hours, you are allowing your brain to be alert, to actually see and experience what is around you. Observation is powerful for business. This type of awareness and connectivity to the world around him helps him write more creative and compelling stories. This type of awareness and connectivity to the world around you could land you a new client and increase revenue in your business.

sales tale:
READ. LOOK FOR CLUES. ACT ON IT.

Another good example of how to find business is to read. I know, no one actually reads anymore. In this world of headlines and clickbait, we have forgotten the value of digging into a good newspaper, magazine, or in-depth online article. I believe in reading as there are clues in articles that inspire me to tweak how I do business, and there are possible prospects in those words I am reading. Many years ago, I was reading *Inc. Magazine*. I still love that magazine and pick up a copy at the airport sometimes when I travel. In the magazine there was a case study about a bunch of CEOs in the clean energy sector. One of the CEOs talked about the power of his large conferences driving his consulting business, so I decided to call him. Again, I went online, got the main number, cold called, and asked for him directly. They transferred me to him. Now, this never happens... I got lucky. BUT, if I were to assume that I'd never get to the CEO on the first try—then I would have never made the call. If I would have never made the call, I would not be booking his meetings as long as I have. (I have been working with this company since 2012.) There was a new CEO, a new meeting planner, and an entire new team, but making the call after reading his words created a new client for me that I still have nine years—and thousands of dollars in commissions—later. Here's how it went:

> **Me:** Hi there, I liked what you said about XYZ in that *Inc. Magazine* article this month. What is the return ratio of success that your conferences are bringing to your consulting business?
>
> **CEO:** (the standard) What, who is this?
>
> **Me:** Mandi with HPN Global and I want to book your meetings. I can help you drive more attendees to your meetings by getting you into

more desirable hotels which will help you continue to increase revenue for your consulting business through your conferences. How important is attendance?

CEO: It's really important, but, how can you do better than I can?

Me: I bet you can find hotels and negotiate the hell out of a contract, there is no doubt in my mind that you can probably do this almost as well as I can (I said being coy and smiling.) *He giggled.* But, wouldn't you rather focus on driving results and building your company? Meetings are just a component of it, and I am a complementary extension of your team. Will you let me ask some questions about your meetings to see if I am a good match for you?

CEO: I guess. Let me connect you to the person currently doing this for me.

Just like that, a warm introduction to the meeting planner— FROM HER BOSS. The CEO and planner are both not at this company anymore, but I still do meetings for the company. And, over the years I have received referrals from the CEO, as well as the planner.

This is all the result of me taking fifteen minutes out of my day to read *Inc. Magazine.* I read it to stimulate my brain, and what a bonus I got when I accidentally found a lead.

Some may say this is stalking, I say it's persistence—and it's my job. Business is everywhere, you just have to pay attention to it. If you keep your antennae up, have a positive attitude, and look for the good, you will find it.

sales tale:
POWER HOUR AND PRIZES

Something I have always done is schedule time in my day, almost every day, to make prospecting phone calls or send prospecting emails. I give myself a goal of fifty dials or twenty emails. I get it done and move on with the rest of the day. When I worked for Hard Rock Hotels, they had a very collaborative work environment and we all worked in cubicles. This was awesome for educational osmosis and training. This was not awesome for focused prospecting calls. I found a "small office" that was more of a broom closet and would lock myself in there to make prospecting calls. I would take my list in, set aside an hour, and focus on just making calls.

When I worked for a large hotel company in Las Vegas, it was during a time when the phones were not ringing. I entered into a situation where seasoned, veteran salespeople now had to make prospecting calls and since business had been so good for so long, they were out of prospecting practice. This was just after the automotive industry crisis of 2008-2010 (which was a part of the financial crisis of 2007-2008 and the resulting Great Recession), and a higher-up political official had said not to go to Las Vegas for your meetings—which caused a very pregnant pause in business. People were afraid of the perception of going to Vegas because some large corporations had been on the news, exposed for their "lavish" meetings in Vegas. It was a weird time to enter a new job, but I took it as a challenge.

This is when I created "Power Hour." Every week on Wednesday, from eight to nine in the morning, we closed our doors, hit the lists, and dialed for dollars. Since I was the ringleader of this troop, I would make ten calls, then make my rounds door-to-door to see if I could help. I'd go back to my office and make ten more calls. I had an electric guitar with a wireless amp from working at Hard Rock Hotels that I would strum loudly at the end of Power Hour. That signaled the team to put their call sheets in the "bin" and the person with the most leads would get a prize. Some days the prize was for "Early Out Friday" (leave work at noon), other days it was a gift certificate for shopping or a bottle of wine. But we always set a time for the calls and rewarded people for the work. We'd reward people for leads. Sometimes I'd reward people for the most calls, or the worst hang up story, or the best engagement story. We'd talk about our Power Hour experiences at the end of the hour for a couple minutes and continue on with our day. This put the whole team back into the practice of looking for business. People could prospect as they wished on their own time throughout the week but this was one time that we all had to do it together, and it worked. I still use Power Hour and Getting In The Closet as tactics in my sales coaching business. This is the first thing we do with any entrepreneur or sales team having problems with time management or building their business. Sometimes I roll my sleeves up and "get into the closet" with them to make calls and give feedback on each call. Sometimes I will rotate with them where I make a call and they make a call and we give each other feedback. The point is to set aside time—even if it's just an hour a week—to build your business. If this is done consistently, without distraction, eventually, the business will come.

sales tale:
TELL PEOPLE YOU LOVE WHAT YOU DO AND EXPLAIN IT

When I first started with HPN, it was tough. It was 100% cold calling and was a 100% commission-based job. I had just left Las Vegas where I produced ten million dollars in one quarter, with my team doing twenty million. My production was 50% of the team, but I could not call on any of my clients because I had signed a non-compete to not talk to clients for one year. I was starting over from scratch, a clean slate. My previous fifteen years of hotel and sales experience mattered, but when I called all my clients the first two days, everyone was already using someone OR they didn't want to use a third party at all. I had to get creative. I drafted an email. I figured my friends and family would want to help. The original version of this email is very lengthy, but it did the trick. My little sister forwarded it to some of her former colleagues, and they forwarded it to some of their colleagues and VOILA—I got a new client. In fact, ten years later, this client is here in town TODAY with her son, and I am having dinner with them tonight. We've done countless meetings together over the years and have become good friends. I also do meetings for her husband, and anyone in her network that she refers to me. The point is, tell your friends and family what you do and how you do it. Don't be shy. Let them know what you need. There is no shame in asking for help. It's better to work with people you know and love, than to cultivate a relationship with a stranger. People want to help you—and sometimes they just need some help understanding what you do, and how you do it.

Here is the original email. But this email sucks, it's too long. Tighten it up and get your point across.

> From: Mandi Kobasic <mkobasic@hpnglobal.com>
> Date: Thu, Sep 16, 2010 at 11:34 AM
> Subject: Networking Nomad Needs Your Help (and you get stuff, too!)
>
> Hi, family!
>
> I am writing today to tell you where in the world Mandi 'Where's Waldo' Kobasic is, and to ask for your help. My new company HPN is a global hotel site selection and consulting firm. This means I can get any hotel in the world for any type of meeting, convention and event. Whether the meeting is in Austin or Alaska, Mumbai (that's fun to say) or Memphis (shout out Ed & Beth!), I can handle the hotels.

If you attend a meeting at a hotel, someone plans that meeting and goes through the grueling task of looking up hotels, finding prices, comparing costs to and from the airport, comparing city taxes and all other costs associated with the meeting. This person typically has a day job full of everyday responsibilities. Finding a hotel for their meeting is a daunting task. In walks Mandi K..............

I simplify the great hotel hunt for them. All they have to do is tell me where they want to go, what price range they'd like to pay, and I take care of the rest. I go to my hotel partners all over the world, get preferred pricing and availability, and zip it back to that person. I also help compare costs and negotiate a contract on behalf of the company/association. Essentially, it saves whomever has to find the hotel tons of time and money. And… It's free!!! The hotel pays me directly so it doesn't cost the meeting organizer or their company/association a dime.

So, if you're chatting with someone planning an event or if you know the contact at your company/association who handles sales meetings, events, annual meetings, conferences, etc. can you pass along my contact info? You can even just forward this email, whatever works best for you.

In addition to my undying gratitude, there will be a prize for anyfamily Kobasic/Waite (or Kobasic/Waite-esque person) to send me a contact name that books. You will receive a gift certificate for a two-night stay to a hotel in your city OR somewhere you've been dying to vacation.

It's easy—get the contact name for the person in charge of hotels next time you're at an event or even for your own company and email it to me. I'll do the rest. If the meeting books, you get a prize (and more of my love! What? It's in demand.)

Thanks for helping me build my business! Thanks for being a great family! Thanks for wanting to win stuff! As Kathy K likes to say, "We're so lucky!"

xo,

Manda

**Feel free to forward this email to anyone you think might want a chance at the prize (and my love)!

Mandi Kobasic

I cringe when I read this email because it's way too long and I don't advocate sending an email this long to anyone—BUT—I think it's worth seeing where it started and how it evolved. I also think there are nuggets in the email above that you can steal and use for your own business.

Below is a revision of the same email I sent out eight years later that ended up getting me a couple more Sales Kick Off Meetings. You will see the email length is the same, but I give the reader an "out." I added a marketing piece where one side showed the meetings I booked, and the other side were testimonials. (See the picture at the end of the chapter.) If people didn't want to continue to read the email, they didn't have to—they could just click on the pretty picture.

REVISED PROSPECTING EMAIL TO FAMILY/ FRIENDS 8 YEARS LATER

From: Mandi Graziano
May 8, 2018
Subject: What In The Heck Does Mandi Graziano Do??

Hi friends. Happy Tuesday. I realize most people don't understand what I do for work, or how I do it. That's my fault, I haven't done a good job of explaining that over the years. I think people know I travel & post cool pics of hotel lobbies but I think the rest gets confusing.

I also realize I have a rad network of family & friends who might be able to benefit from using my services. I am making a big push to grow my business this year and since referrals mean everything to me, here is a shameless email asking for referrals from my friends and family :)

If you don't want to read the rest of this super long email, click on the attachment—see testimonials from happy customers, forward it, or send me some meetings to book. OR... keep reading below... if you dare...

I book meetings at hotels. Meetings can be as small as ten, or as large as you want.

Examples of meetings I've booked:

- Quarterly Business Review for 40 in Bermuda
- President Club/Incentive Trips for 200 in Aruba, Cancun, Costa Rica
- User's Conference for 400 in San Diego
- Pediatric Medical Association for 2000 in San Antonio
- Technology Product Launch for 200 in Stockholm
- Engineering meeting for 100 in Bangkok.
- Investigator Medical Meetings for 30 in Chicago, Dallas and Palo Alto.
- I have even booked cheerleading, soccer and basketball tournaments for youth sports leagues. *Really—anytime anyone needs a hotel for 10 people or more...I can help.*

There is no cost to you. The hotel pays me a commission directly.

How it works:

- Give me meeting/event/conference dates, number of rooms per night, meeting space, destination
- I source it for you and produce a report within 48 hours
- You short list your top 2
- I negotiate best and final offers and contracts
- I turn over to you to plan
- If you don't have someone to plan the meeting, I have a planning team that can do it for you. (There is a cost to have my team plan it.)
- If you are unfamiliar with the hotel I set up a site inspection for you. If you don't have time, I will do a site inspection for you, or we can set up a virtual tour.

Call to Action:

- If you want my help, shoot me an email.
- If you attend conferences & think they can be better, send me the name of the event and I can find the contact person from there.
- If you know someone that could use my help, forward this email.

In exchange, if you have a business you're pedaling, let me know how I can help you grow your business. What do you offer? Maybe I have some referrals for you???

I love helping my friends achieve their goals and thrive in life, so let me know how I can help you!

Thanks for being wonderful people in my life, and for reading this email.

Thanks in advance for any referrals that come my way. Have a MARVELOUS May!

Mandi Graziano
Vice President Global Accounts
Hospitality Performance Network Global,
mgraziano@hpnglobal.com

Shortly after I sent this email, my mom was eavesdropping on some people in the waiting room of the mechanic's shop (she must have read my earlier sales tale on the importance of eavesdropping—good job, mom!) In the hour she was there she quickly determined the name of an association having a meeting, why they were unhappy with their current location, and where they have always wanted to go. She texted me with great excitement. I quickly investigated said association, called the executive director and asked, "Have you ever wanted to go to Miami for your meeting?" It was like Big Brother was watching—but Big Brother was my mama. That was enough for me to be able to set up a demo call and the rest is history. This simple email that I sent to friends and family turned into a slew of new customers and eventually referrals, not to mention lifelong friendships and relationships. If you think people in your circle don't care about what you do, you're wrong. People may not care about your work or understand your job but they care about you and want to see you succeed. If you share what you do and ask specifically for help, they will provide. And, in turn, give them the same. For every lead I get from a family or friend I ask how I can return the favor, and I do. Make good on your word and thank people—even your mom and your sister—for referrals. They are what grows your business.

THE LESSONS:

1. Keep your antennae up everywhere.
2. Make time to read to look for business.
3. Tell people you love about what you do. Ask for help.
4. Get involved with neighboring businesses and within your community.
5. Eavesdropping and spreading good rumors about your business is good.

This is the marketing flyer that was attached to my "Friends and Family Prospecting Email." I got the idea for this piece from a local realtor who sent recent home sales and prices on one side and a funny picture of he and his kids on the other. I added the testimonials for "kicks."

" Mandi is my secret weapon. She's relentless.

"Thank you for your doggedness and tenacity"

"She's so good. I suspect she uses sorcery. She made my life easier and I never got turned into an amphibian."

"Your support in getting hotels to pay attention to my meeting is so valuable. I was used to negotiating with hotel sales teams directly... but you do it so much better."

 HOTEL SOURCING

 SITE SELECTION

 CONTRACT NEGOTIATION

 MEETING MANAGEMENT

MANDI GRAZIANO, VICE PRESIDENT GLOBAL ACCOUNTS, HPN GLOBAL
MGRAZIANO@HPNGLOBAL.COM

RECENTLY BOOKED
MEETINGS

PRESIDENT'S CLUB TRIP	CITYWIDE CONVENTION	ANNUAL MEDICAL ASSOCIATION MEETING
CABO SAN LUCAS	SAN JOSE CA	CHICAGO IL
40 GUESTS	2,000 ATTENDEES	1,200 ATTENDEES

OPERATIONS MEETING TECHNOLOGY COMPANY	CORPORATE TRADE SHOW	CUSTOMER CONFERENCE
NASHVILLE TN	HAMBURG GERMANY	HELSINKI FINLAND
30 PEOPLE	250 ATTENDEES	400 PEOPLE

FOOD SERVICE ASSOCIATION ANNUAL MEETING	TECHNOLOGY USER'S CONFERENCE	TOP PERFORMER'S INCENTIVE
FT. WORTH TX	SAN DIEGO CA	COSTA RICA
500 ATTENDEES	300 ATTENDEES	250 PEOPLE

i collect people...

Networking is more than hobnobbing and schmoozing at happy hours. It comes in many shapes and sizes. It can happen over years. Be open to how you meet people. Networking is an opportunity to start a conversation with someone that may continue for years into the future. - Mandi-ism

Networking is such a lame word. However, it's a necessity in all avenues of life. If you want to get a new job, you must network. If you want to get feedback on the school you want your kids to get into, you have to network. If you want to open dialogue about your product or service, you must network. Networking is not always something that gregarious people do at a happy hour over a couple cocktails. Networking is not transactional. Good networking is not about instant gratification. Networking happens in many forms—from workouts to weddings, backyards to boardrooms. You can meet someone once and that person can be in your life forever in many different ways. That is networking. If you are the type of person with social anxiety and conjuring up a conversation with a stranger is petrifying to you, don't worry, you too can network. It doesn't always have to feel like a sales pitch—or even be a sales pitch. It can be a quick introduction from someone in your family or social circle that drops a nugget of information that plants a seed. If you plant seeds and surround yourself with like-minded people that are aligned with your beliefs, your community will grow over time. Networking is more than just business; it's growing a community that helps you move your life forward in a productive and joyful way.

sales tale:
HOW CHASING THE OLYMPIC TORCH THROUGH THE STREETS OF SAN FRANCISCO MADE ME A BETTER NETWORKER

In April 2008, I went to San Francisco for a client networking baseball game. I ended up running with protestors looking for the Olympic Torch. My event was at seven in the evening at Oracle Stadium (formerly AT&T). I arrived in the city earlier that day and had some errands to run. For some reason there was a requirement that all the salespeople wear matching outfits. The outfit I was supposed to wear—but did not have— was a white t-shirt with a white cardigan. In the spirit of sales unity, I complied and set out to find a damn white cardigan as soon as I got to the city. I walked from my hotel about two miles to The Gap. Surely they would have a white cardigan, and they did. BOOM. The first one I tried on worked. I was golden. Now all I had to do was briskly walk back to my hotel, do some work for a couple hours, strap on my white upper gear and head to the baseball field. Boy was I wrong. I never could have guessed how the next two hours would unfold. As I walked out of The Gap, I noticed crowds of people forming lines on the street as if they were waiting for something.

I asked someone, "What is all the raucous all about?"

"Oh, the Olympic torch is being run through San Francisco on it's way to Beijing for the Olympics."

"Cool, where's it going?"

"We don't know. Maybe over there..."

He pointed to a terribly busy street that didn't seem blocked off for such a monumental run. I was skeptical. I continued to walk down the street and somehow got tousled up with a wild band of protesters. They were fighting with another wild band of protesters. Each group had its own flag, and they were running fast, carrying their flags and flag fighting. It looked like they were each using their little flag poles as swords. They were running extremely fast as if they were chasing someone or something. I didn't know what to do, but was curious, and had two hours to kill before the game, so I ran with them. We ran up and down so many hills in San Francisco. The run was aimless and as we wound around the streets, each group was screaming at the other group. I couldn't make out the words they were using but they sounded really mad. I ran with them hoping to see the Olympic torch, but all I saw were protesters and counter protesters who looked like mice in a maze with no end destination. The streets were so full—there were people arriving for the Giants game and the standard insanity of a busy city—with people walking everywhere and cars stopped, beeping at us and each other. I ran with one group for a bit and then switched to the other group. They were all so wayward. There was no route. They were angry. It was dangerous. I loved every minute of it.

After about an hour of this nonsense, I gave up and went back to my hotel room for a much-needed rinse off before heading to the game. When I got to the game, in the fancy suite at Giants Stadium, I was sharing my experience with one of the potential clients. He seemed jealous and envious of the story. I didn't realize why until he laid out the back story, the real reason this was happening. While I was running with the protesters, I had assumed these wild wolf packs of flag carriers were just each proud of their own country, and running to look for the Olympic Torch carrier. I was wrong.

My potential client told me that protest group number one were China supporters & protest group number two were Tibet supporters. At that time, there was upheaval about the way China was treating Tibet and Sudan, and since the Olympics were in Beijing that year, there were protests in every city. My super smart potential client also shared with me that San Francisco was the only stop for the torch in North America that year. I asked him about the torch route because it seemed like the yahoos I was with didn't have any idea where they were going. He said, "That's because they changed the torch route this morning after the opening ceremonies.

No one knew where the torch was going and everyone was looking for it all day." Apparently, the protest threat was so bad that the city cut the distance in half, changed the route to avoid protesters, and the poor torch man was hiding in a warehouse somewhere near the water. I had been flying from San Diego to San Francisco when this was shared in the news and had no idea this was about to happen. I was just living it, LIVE, in real time. The potential client said that he was trying to get off work all day to look for the torch and be a part of the excitement, but he couldn't make it happen. He was really interested to hear about what I saw, play by play. I had no idea I was experiencing such a desired moment.

My torch run with the protesters sparked an awesome conversation with the potential new client. We talked about the Olympics, his thoughts about China, Tibet, yoga, zen moments—and all sorts of other topics that would never have come up had I not told the story of the day. I learned, in that moment, that my client is a news and current events buff. He knew everything about the crowds, the number of protesters, and what the police were doing to keep everyone safe. I learned at that moment that he was a facts and numbers junkie. This would later help me when we eventually started working together. If I would have just shown up to that event, in my white cardigan, talking about mundane things like the weather or our jobs, I never would have created a deeper connection with a potential client. Now, I am not saying to go find yourself a protest in a new city every time you travel somewhere for work. I am saying, open yourself up at these networking events. Share a little—even if it's unusual—so you can get to a deeper level of connection with people. I still remember that moment, that conversation, and that client. We are still friends and business associates and it all started because I shared a wacky story.

sales tale:
TABLE EIGHT IS GREAT

One time I crashed a wedding and gained a client. I was the guest of a friend at a wedding for two people I had never met. They were nice, and seemed happy that I was crashing their very intimate wedding of less than fifty people. I was seated at table eight. It was a magical evening in San Diego. The bride and groom got married on the beach at sunset. We followed them from the beach to a gorgeous beachfront house for the reception and dinner. The sun was setting, the sky was pink, the temperature was perfect outside. The patio was set with round tables and twinkling lights which made the environment perfect for strangers to get to know each other. Our table was the best by far. I met two lady lawyers and their husbands and I lost track of my date. One of their husbands was writing a book so we kibitzed for quite a bit. I taught the lady lawyers how to "break the line"—which is a tactic used for trying to look skinnier in pictures—and we took many photos of us trying it out. We danced and then reconvened at table eight for more pictures, conversations, and laughter.

Immediately after the wedding we all became Facebook friends and several months later, one of the guys sent me a sample from his book. I read it. It was good. We lost touch over the years but always saw each other's Facebook posts. Five or so years later I got a message from one of the guys and he told me he was recently given the project of hosting a meeting for his company. He asked me if that is something I knew how to do. I told him—of course— that I'd love to help. I was even more excited that they were looking at San Diego which meant I got to reunite with them. I sourced his meeting. They came out to review the hotels and we all had a swell reunion. After all these years, he is still my client. Every time we do a new contract for a new meeting, we both agree, in an email, "Table eight is great."

I'm not saying you should wear your profession as a badge wherever you go. Those people are annoying and that is just plain weird. I am saying that posting a couple of hotel pics on Facebook and just being a friendly human being helped me gain a new client and make new memories with my table eight mates.

I have some rules for myself around networking. They may not work for you, but I challenge you to find a different way of connecting with people. I find networking events so boring sometimes and I want to have real, meaningful conversations with people—or at least have a laugh. Leaving your home and traveling somewhere is such hard work and I believe in making the best and most of these moments.

Rule #1: Never talk about the weather. For God's sake, if you talk to me about the weather in your first sentence—I AM OUT. That is a signal for a lame, boring, human with nothing creative or interesting to say. Think about your interactions, let your guard down—these are humans, so get to know each other and try to find common ground. An exception to this rule is if you or your client are farmers or your business is impacted by weather, such as a storm, hurricane, fire, or impending tsunami (but these are the only "talk about the weather" exceptions).

Rule #2: Read the local newspaper. When going to another city for business, read the local newspaper that morning to discover the hot topics in your potential client's world. (Had I done this in April 2008, I would have been a little more informed of my accidental protest run!)

Rule #3: SWEATworking. I've attended many spin classes, brisk walks, volleyball games, and hikes with business partners and clients. There is a reason why people say golf is a good game to learn if you want to go into business—it's a long game. You learn the other person's strengths or weaknesses. You learn how they think and their strategy. You see how they behave when they are at their best and worst. And you have plenty of time to get to know someone, out of the shop, board room, or office. People are different when you remove them from their normal, boring work setting.

Rule #4: Remember the color of their eyes. Whenever I go into an event cold, where I know absolutely no one, I try to remember the name of each person I meet. I look into their

eyes when I meet them, give them a firm handshake and try
to remember the color of their eyes. James, green eyes. Kim,
blue eyes. Mike, one eye. Remembering the color of their eyes
and their name helps me remember them. Another thing I
try to do in that quick conversation is repeat their name 3
times. *Danielle, nice to meet you. So, Danielle, tell me about
your business, what does XYC company do? Danielle, what do
you think about the Cleveland Browns this year?* I don't rapid-
fire the name in the first three sentences. I try to spread it over
a five- or ten-minute conversation. That helps me remember
their name and makes the experience more personal. She may
remember me as a creepy, leering, eyeball-looker, but at least
she remembers me, right?

Rule #5: Work the room. I know this is cliché but it's really
important to maximize time. You're only there for two hours
or less so make the most of your time. Try to get to know as
many people as possible while balancing your conversations so
they are still quality, meaningful conversations.

**Rule #6: I never give my business card unless someone asks
me for one.** I do ask for business cards if I want to get to
know the person or their business more. When I was younger,
I used to just hand out business cards like candy. I was super
annoying. I have learned over the years that if people are
interested in you or your business, they will ask—or track you
down. Forcing your card on someone will ensure it ends up
in the trash.

Rule #7: Smile, have fun, look for the good. I love meeting
new people. I love strangers. If you don't like meeting people

or strangers, then you need to find a business development person to do the networking for you. There is no shame in being a shy business owner. Keep doing what you're doing with your awesome widget or service. But your company needs to be out there, mixing in public. People need to know who your business is so find someone who likes strangers as much as I do. Even if the networking event was a bust—meaning you didn't find any potential clients—maybe there was a recommendation for a book or movie, or a tip on putting your kids to bed. Networking events are not transactional. It's rare you will go to an event and leave with three leads for new business. Networking events are the beginning of a relationship you can build, grow, and foster so it leads to new business.

Rule #8: Be open to learning about other people's products too. I always remember that even though I am there to find business and meet new people, other people are there for the same reason. If I am a target for someone's sales plan, I do not run away—this networking thing goes both ways. I give people the time they deserve to get to know me, sell to me, and share their values and business ideas with me. You never know, someday that person might eventually be a client or business associate—or maybe even your boss, boyfriend, stepson or mother-in-law. I always try to be kind and open to all people at a networking event because you never know where that relationship will go.

Mikey G's Tale:

I've known Mikey G for almost twenty years. We were salespeople at a hotel together in San Diego. We had the same job, but we handled different markets. I remember when our sales offices were being renovated and the leadership team crammed all the salespeople into one banquet room for a couple of weeks. It was during the winter, which meant everyone had a cold. It was gross and felt like a germ dome. Mike and I escaped from the sniffle box and created our own work room in the basement of the hotel. We had a huge white board and developed so many awesome ideas in that non-germy room together. We feverishly wrote ideas on the big white board about how we could bring new clients to the hotel. We worked really well together, bouncing ideas off one another. We complemented each other's skill sets. Mike was always ahead of his time. He pitched so many great ideas to the hotel to increase business but the hotel just wasn't set up or ready for his ideas yet. The hotel wanted to do things the way they always had done them and Mike's innovative ideas to bring in new types of business fell on deaf ears. Eventually, Mike moved to a different area of hospitality where his creative mind and operational excellence was appreciated and could flourish. Eventually, I moved on to work for Mikey G in that same environment. Networking with Mike in the non-germy room in the basement of the hotel many years ago was the beginning of a very long, and awesome, business relationship. We were first co-workers, then Mike became my boss, and now I am his client and he's in my book. You never know where these business relationships will take you. So when you meet someone interesting, that you respect and adore, hold onto that because you never know how that relationship will develop and change and how the two of you can help each other.

"Mandi is fearless in developing new relationships and connecting people. She never wastes an opportunity to work a room and never squanders her chance to connect two people if she thinks they should meet. She will yield some benefit from each conversation even if she gets nothing out of it for herself but it advances others. After fifteen years in the restaurant management business, my single best account came from a call that came from Mandi that started with, "You have to meet this guy, you two will hit it off," and she was right."

Mike Georgopoulos, Partner, RMD Group.

sales tale:
NETWORKING EVENT
THAT WENT AWRY

It was very early in my career and I went to a networking event. I was in my mid-twenties and I brought a gal pal along with me. The food and drink were flowing like the San Diego River after a rare rain. I got so drunk that I acted like I was at a party, and not a business function. I started talking to a guy who I thought was handsome. We were eating sushi. I was using chopsticks and he was shoving sushi in his mouth with his hands. (Red Flag #1.) He was a DJ for corporate events and an MC, so he had a great voice. He seemed genuinely nice so when he asked for my number, I gave it to him.

Later that week he called me for a date and we were to go out the following Friday. All week long my roommate (the gal I brought to the event) was razzing me about going out with the guy that ate sushi with his hands. She said he seemed too old for me and gross. (Red Flag #2.) I ignored her. The date approached and as twenty-five-year olds do, I cancelled. I wanted to hang out with my friends instead of going on a date with him. After I cancelled, he called me on my landline twenty-three times. Each message he left got more and more aggressive. *How dare you cancel on me. You bitch, you stupid fucking bitch. I am going to kill you. You will never cancel on me again.* In between the angry voice messages he would just call and hang up. I called the police. The police called him and he never called again. I saw him leering at me from afar at a trade show years later. I got scared and had the police walk me to my car. I never saw him again.

As much as I love people and networking, this was an experience that made it clear to me that exercising some caution during networking is important. This guy obviously was not a good business partner, or a good potential suitor. Tell people the area you live in, rather than the street. Give people your work email, not your personal cell phone number. And, if you can help it, try not to get too drunk at networking events. And be careful about accepting dates from people in a work setting unless you have fully vetted them and it won't disrupt your business practice. Most importantly, if you meet a potential suitor or business associate eating sushi with their hands, run like hell.

CHAPTER THREE

don't propose
on the first date

You don't normally propose on the first date, that would be creepy. Expecting someone to sign on the dotted line the first day you meet them is weird too. Developing and building relationships takes time. -Mandi-ism

Building and maintaining business relationships is hard. Everyone is so busy with their own interests. Our family and friends keep us busy. Our job keeps us busy. What's left? Not much. But nurturing relationships is the key to a fruitful sales career. You do not have to be the type of person constantly reaching out. However, you do have to be the type of person interested in other people. I don't mean that you need to be creepy and drill people with questions because you're "supposed" to. I do mean that you should be curious about the people in your sphere. Ask them open-ended questions.

Wonder what excites them or makes them angry. All of this isn't done in the first, second, or even the third meeting.

Having deep relationships with customers takes a long time. You may have a customer now that didn't like you at first. However, over time, once you got to know each other, I bet you found common ground that made you accept and understand each other a little more. I've never been a fan of the saying, "People buy from people they like." I disagree with this statement. I think we might be interested in a product that someone we like is selling, but ultimately, I won't buy it just because I like them. I must like the product first and I do have to *trust* the person selling it. I believe that people buy from people they trust. How do you create a relationship where enough trust develops for someone to buy from you? TIME! Time is a beautiful thing and trust is not built overnight. Would you marry a person you only went on one date with? It just doesn't happen like that—at least not all of the time. You can't have one quick call or one quick interaction with someone then rush to ask them for the business. I mean, you can, but it will be a better, more stable relationship if you build it over time and exercise patience. Even after you have secured the business, you have to keep building the relationship because things change over time. I've found that by being authentic, asking honest and open-ended questions (where I am genuinely curious about the answers), and infusing memorable creativity along the way, are the best ways to establish and maintain long-term business and personal relationships.

Julie's Tale:

Julie and I worked together at a hotel almost twenty years ago. We still work together now at HPN Global. She brought me over to "the other side" almost eleven years ago. I will forever be grateful to her saying to me, "Mandi, you've been on the hotel side too long. It's time to move on." Julie is like my big sister who tells it like it is. She doesn't like to hug, but I make her hug me anyway. Our relationship didn't start with hugs and happiness. We met when she found a bigger piece of business at the hotel and bumped my group out of the hotel. This could have been a bad start to a relationship. She was much more senior and more experienced than I was at the time. She could have just trampled over my business and said, "Take that junior!" but she didn't. Instead, she wrote me a beautiful handwritten note apologizing for having to move my group, and thanking me for understanding the bigger picture. At the time, I did not understand the business lesson, but a couple years later, I would get that message. In subsequent conversations with Julie that same year, she continued to explain business strategy to me and was patient with my many questions. We stayed in touch over the years and we still have a monthly catch-up call. This is an important relationship to me because Julie has been a mentor, a sounding board and a fun human to have in my life. My career would not be the same without her.

"If Building Relationships was in the dictionary, there would be a photograph of Mandi Graziano. Whether it's at a restaurant or with her clients, Mandi knows how to listen and ask critical questions to genuinely understand who people are."

Julie Dunkle, Co-Founder NYX Endurance.

sales tale:

YOU HAVE TO LOVE WHAT YOU DO TO BUILD GOOD RELATIONSHIPS

I got fired from my second sales job. I worked for an office solutions company. *What does that even mean?* That was the problem. I didn't understand what I was selling and I didn't like what I was selling. I was afraid and embarrassed to talk about it in public or to potential customers. It was also my first job out of college. My look was wrong. My clothes were wrong. I was a young girl in an office full of seasoned professionals and no one really liked me. I don't blame them, I was weird. I still am, but at that time I had no experience and couldn't hide behind professional success. I was just weird, inexperienced, and selling a product I didn't like with people that didn't like me. My boss made us read this lame book. (Trust me, it wasn't as funny as this one.) There were references to war, Ulysses S. Grant, and some odd shit about the competition that I believe could have been illustrated much differently. We had weekly meetings in my boss' office and had to do a chapter-by-chapter book report. I lied, and said I read the book. I know he knew I was lying. He was understandably frustrated with me. We were all in cubicles and when I would cold call clients I would whisper. I even had a couple potential clients say, "I can't hear you." I'd whisper because I wasn't confident about what I was saying on the phone. I didn't really understand what we were selling and didn't really understand the company. It was an impossible sell for me to articulate. I'd hang up when I felt awkward—which happened in the middle of a call sometimes.

I knew we had a huge print warehouse. I knew one of my colleagues was doing all the catalogue printing for Victoria's Secret and a big cosmetics company. I knew she had won the account and it was a big deal for the company. I didn't understand how she went about scoring the business or convincing people to let us print the catalogue. I just knew the catalogue was really pretty and there were a lot of fancy glossy colors in it. Even after I asked the successful salesperson how she scored the deal, I didn't understand her answer or process. I was completely out of my league with a product I was not interested in.

My territory was the eastern suburbs of Cleveland which was the heart of manufacturing in northeast Ohio at that time. I remember driving around with my boss and he would point to buildings and say, "See that building, there's a lot of printing that goes on in there. Let's see how they do it." We'd get out of the car, march up to the reception desk and give them our business cards. We'd ask, "Who handles your printing?" and then we'd never get an appointment. Each time we got back in the car, I was in charge of writing the building number down and the names of all the businesses in that building. This would eventually become a prospecting list. This is still a practice I use that has become valuable. When I am at the doctor's office or the massage therapist, I take a picture of the other businesses in that building and research them to see if they are potential prospects.

However, in this job, I never once saw a full sales process from start to finish. I think it's important for new salespeople to see the lifecycle of at least three sales during their training. This way, newbies can keep tabs on the process to understand the twists and turns a sale can take. In this role, I only saw fragmented parts of the sale with different people. I needed to see the whole picture so I could truly understand the business. I saw a variety of people go on sales calls and make cold calls.

One time I was shadowing one of the salespeople who was clearly an alcoholic. I didn't know this at the time, but looking back, it seems clear to me now. Her whole car smelled like cigarettes, farts, and whiskey. We would go to see a client and when the client would shake her hand, they backed up a bit as if they did not like her scent. That cigarette/fart/whiskey combo permeated her whole being. I watched her interact with clients and she was vacant. There was no connection.

It was transactional. She made dumb small talk for a couple minutes, like the weather, then went right into popping the abrupt, out-of-sync question, "What do you have for me?" The transition was odd for me and the client, but not for the salesperson. She was there to get something from someone and move on. Sometimes she would get the print order, but most times she wouldn't. We'd go to the next place, and it was the same thing.

In between calls we stopped at her house for her to go to the bathroom. It was so strange to be sitting in some weird lady's kitchen while she drops a number two and then head back out. I am assuming it was a number two because of the length of time in the bathroom, and the lingering fart smell. We had three meals a day with clients. She drank at all of them. I am surprised I wasn't afraid to be a passenger in her car because by the end of the sales day, she was hammered. She spit when she talked. Her makeup ran down her face and she had a twitch in her left eye. She did make an attempt at mouthwash one day, but all I could smell was booze, cigarettes, and farts. Although this was a weird experience, I did learn a lot from these visits with her.

I learned that your physical impression is important:

- How you look and speak in the first twenty seconds of meeting someone has a lasting effect.

- I learned how important it is to carry Altoids or a Listerine Breath Strip when on business appointments.

- I learned that even though I am a "shine from the inside out" type person, most people are not. Most people are sizing you up the minute they meet you. Shabby clothes, a shrunken posture, a grumpy face and boozy breath can all be reasons someone decides not to work with you.

- Throw your shoulders back, smile and be proud when first meeting someone. *Authentic enthusiasm is contagious.* When this salesperson first greeted people, she'd give them a limp hand shake and say, "Hey, so what I'm thinking is..." She jumped right into it. It was a little off putting.

Aside from the smoky fart face lady, I shadowed other salespeople. There was the lady with the "schoolteacher" style. I really liked her approach and clients instantly trusted her. I know she did not like me and was annoyed she had to spend the day with me. Her approach with clients was that of an educator. She asked a lot of open-ended questions. When the customer answered, she addressed their questions specifically and educated them as to why our service was good for them. She always walked away with a print order. She also had a technique that I really liked and still use. She always had a pad of paper with her in the meeting and took ferocious notes. After each meeting, she immediately rushed to the car and wrote down specific notes about the client. *Two kids, baseball tournaments on weekends, from Florida, divorced, next print job in four months, new training director, get name.* Then she meticulously followed up on each of her notes. At the time,

Outlook wasn't a thing, and CRMs (Customer Relationship Management systems) were archaic. I saw her flip page-by-page through her paper planner, writing each follow-up note for weeks and months ahead. I still do this—but using Outlook or my CRM. I overheard her on the phone on a Monday calling the same customer we just saw on the previous Friday saying, "How was the weekend? Did the boys win or lose their games?" She was solid. She had big brown eyes and round glasses. She looked like a wise owl and she fit the mold of one too. I can't remember her name, but I do remember her technique.

There was another girl who was the cool girl in the office. She was pretty, dressed stylishly with an edge, had a raspy voice, and always cracked jokes. When we'd walk through the print warehouse everyone loved her. She'd high five all the print operators and customer service reps. When she was on the phone with a customer, she took the "best gal pal" approach. She'd say, "Hey, what's up? What's on tap for the weekend?" She engaged with people like they were her buddies. She was chummy with everyone—internal and external customers. She also left appointments with print jobs. I liked her approach because she disarmed people. People felt comfortable with her, and they really liked her. She was fun to go on sales calls with—we'd sing songs loudly in her car. I learned the value of mutual respect for co-workers (the internal customer), by watching her interact with the company's operators. They are the people activating the sale which is why it's so important to have a solid relationship with your crew. She did a great job of modeling that for me.

I did have one person who liked me at this job. She was my mentor—steady Freddy. This was her first sales job, but she had been doing it for twenty years. Her previous job was a dental appointment scheduler. She got this job because in the interview she told the boss, "I had to convince people to come in for a root canal and each day the calendar had to be filled with appointments or I'd get fired. If I can sell people into getting a root canal, I can sell your print projects." I appreciated her perspective, after all, that was a good point. She didn't have a "sales-y" personality at all. Her voice was soft and low. She was calm and charming. Everyone she met felt at ease with her and she really knew what she was talking about. She was more of a therapist/counselor-type than she was a salesperson. She went into each appointment knowing that the client had a problem. She listened—man oh man, did she listen! Her appointments were really long but they were quality appointments. She left each appointment with multiple print jobs and at least three referrals. She asked good questions and people opened up to her. There were many appointments where she'd end up holding the client's hand, gazing into their eyes assuring them that she'd help them and make their life easier. I didn't feel like we sold print jobs with her. I felt like she was Oprah, or a shaman, or a psychic healer. She was highly effective. I learned a lot about that approach. If time is our greatest asset, and we spend a lot of time with one customer, we better make it count. Make the relationship matter for both of you so there is a long-term possibility of working together.

Imagine me, twenty-two years old, fresh out of college, not understanding what I was selling, being a fly on the wall to all these salespeople—just observing all these relationship-building tactics. It all felt and looked so strange to me because I had never been in that position. After weeks of shadowing I still couldn't get my spiel down. I couldn't call customers without being embarrassed. I didn't know what to say when I'd meet a customer face-to-face. I never came back to the office with print jobs.

They eventually sent me away to official "Sales Training." It was some of the best training I received in my life. Even after twenty-five years in sales—both receiving and delivering good training throughout this time—this program was still the top. The cast of characters there was a rough batch of "plebes" just like me, new to the company. We traveled to somewhere in Texas for a two-day sales seminar and they grouped us in teams of three. My team was an old guy who has been selling other things for years. He was new to this industry but not new to sales, and he told us so. He was brash, rude, called us "darling," "sweetie," and "honey" and believed he knew more than anyone in the class. He was a big man, standing at least six feet four and weighing in at nearly three hundred pounds. His voice was deep and muffled like he had a whole chicken stuck in his throat. He was hairy—and smelly, like farts and smoke again. (Why do all these old salespeople smell like farts?) The other girl had never sold anything in her life. She was an academic. She was from Canada and had the accent to boot. There was a lot of "eh" and "sorry" in her vocabulary and she had just finished getting her master's in organizational psychology. I was confused as to why she had this job.

The three of us were a motley crew. Each exercise we did at our table went awry. Chicken throat would talk too much. Canadian needed time to process everything. I was the peacemaker between the two. We were behind in all of our assignments because we wasted a bunch of time debating what we should do and how we should do it. The big message of the training was to listen and ask open-ended questions. When someone gave you an answer, you were supposed to ask another question, and another question, and another question. I liked this technique. I saw how it got people to be open and you learned so much more about the person, their buying habits and their business. It was our final day of training after many exhausting sessions of listening, asking questions, and peacemaking. It was time for each group to make a presentation. I can't remember the topic of the presentation but something life-changing happened that would alter the course of my career forever. The highly-educated Canuck was to be the speaker of our group while Smelly Chicken Throat was going to chime in with his "sales experience." Since I was the youngest and most inexperienced, I was relegated to taking notes and observing the audience for buy signals and cues. Each team was supposed to bring a problem to the table and show how we solved it. Canuck got up there, the shining academic star of the whole training class… and she froze. She literally froze. She stood there, blankly staring at the audience and no words came out of her mouth. People were shocked. I was shocked. Our team was screwed. She shook her head, turned away and ran off the stage and started crying. Smelly Chicken Throat stood up and said, "She was the one that did all the research on this so I don't know what to tell you." Then he waddled off the stage.

The two of them were loudly arguing in the background. At this moment, I don't know what came over me but I went to the stage. Words just started flowing out of my mouth about Johannes Guttenberg and the first printing press and how we need to pivot to be relevant. Modern day printing is not much different than it was in the fifteenth century... blah blah blah. I had no idea what I was saying. I felt like a parent from the Peanuts gang—I saw my body and my mouth moving and a bunch of garbled nonsense came out. It must have made sense because when I was done, the audience started clapping. They asked me questions and I had some answers, but not all of them. With the questions I could not answer I said, "Great question, what makes this answer important to you?" And then that information helped me dive deeper into their needs so I was eventually able to solve their problem. I got off the stage, sweaty, and my teammates rallied around me thanking me for stepping in and improvising. Our sales trainer grabbed the three of us and made us take a walk. He asked two simple questions to which I still use to this day when there is a conflict in business and in life. First question, "What happened?" It's such a simple question, but there is room for so much in the answer. Each person had their own version of what happened. Next question, "Why?" He tilted his head—like when a dog wants a biscuit—and he looked deeply into our eyes as if he wanted to really know *why?*

Everyone had their own version of "Why?" Canuck was frustrated at the speed and carelessness of Chicken Throat. Canuck was in analysis paralysis. She couldn't make a decision about anything because she was overthinking everything and overwhelmed by data and the team personality. That caused her to freeze and, ultimately, not do her job. Chicken Throat didn't want to work on a team with two young girls as he felt it was beneath him. I just wanted everyone to get along, and since we weren't, it was very difficult for me. Our team issues had nothing to do with sales. It had everything to do with personalities and perspective. We all had our own perspective. No one was listening to the other person. Not one of us was trying to share responsibilities or understand the other person's point of view. We all looked at the project in a silo without realizing that we couldn't get anything done without working together, as a team. He commended me for stepping up for the team even though I didn't understand all the content and gave some incorrect info about the history of the printing press.

I learned in that moment that the value of making a decision—even if it's not the best decision—instead of being paralyzed by deliberation was valuable. I still stand by that principle. There are so many moments in life where you have to make a quick decision without all the data needed and you don't have enough time to think it through. The best decision to make at that moment is to make any decision, it may not be the best one, but at least it's a decision. You can always fix it later, and learn from the mistake—if it happens to be a bad decision. As a result of me improvising at that moment, I walked away from that training class with the Most Likely To

Succeed trophy. I actually got an award for a company that I didn't like, where I wasn't liked. When I went back to work the next Monday, my boss' boss gave me a big shout out and everyone was shocked. I was shocked too, but I like trophies so I took it.

We all went back to work after the sales meeting and I assumed I'd get on the phones like a champ and sell all the print jobs. I couldn't do it. I slipped back into my old ways. I whispered. I was embarrassed to talk in public about what we did. I was ashamed that I was successful in Texas but not at home. I didn't make my numbers and as a result I was fired a couple of weeks later. I learned a valuable lesson from this—I wasn't proud of what I was selling and didn't understand it. When you're not passionate about your product, you can't sell it. When you don't understand what you're selling, no one is going to buy from you. If you can deliver a quick sentence about your business, product or service, when it rolls off your tongue, then you're in the right space. If you can't, then get out—quick.

The trainer saw something in me that I hadn't seen in myself. He saw my ability to improvise and to make a quick decision in a business crisis. He probably knew I wasn't the right fit for the print sales company but he saw me ask questions, listen, and offer a solution. Whatever product or service you're selling, these three things will help you win and sustain the business. For years after that I was obsessed with asking questions—and still am. All open-ended questions. I practiced twenty-four hours a day turning all yes-or-no questions into open-ended questions. I made it a game. All I wanted were long answers where people would give me loads of information. The more info, the better. Although I got fired from that job for not performing, I was exposed to so many different sales techniques. I also got a trophy, and I learned the lesson that if you are not truly passionate about your product, people know it and they won't buy from you so you won't have the chance to build a relationship.

shawna's tale:

I met Shawna when I was nineteen years old. We went to college together and at that time, we could not have been more different. Shawna wore business suits to class. I wore the same thing every day—a sweatshirt and dirty jeans. Somehow we built a relationship based on common interests such as driving around in her car listening to "Verbal Advantage" tapes. We loved hearing a vocabulary word, the origin, saying it in a sentence then using that word together all week in various settings— at our sorority meetings, in class, at a bar, or at a frat house. Shawna is one of the most interesting relationships I have and she is one of the most interesting relationship builders I know. She stood up in front of our sorority at age nineteen and said, "OK girls, today I am going to teach you about an IRA. From now until you are fifty-nine and a half you will give me money once a month. You will thank me later when you are millionaires." So, I did. I've been giving her some sort of money every month since I was nineteen. She was an intern for a financial company at the time and was learning how to prospect and build relationships. Even as an intern, Shawna had the vision to tap into her entire network to build her business. I don't know who else invested with Shawna back then, but I am glad I did. Since then she has built an amazingly successful wealth advisory business and consistently wins awards. She has a way about her where she listens and is genuinely interested in everything you have to say. I've learned a lot over the years watching her interact with people and curiously ask questions about different people's interests. Although they may be completely different from Shawna, she embraces that knowledge and finds ways to connect, just like she did with me and my dirty jeans back in the 90s. I am also proud to call her one of my best friends. I still wear sweatshirts and dirty jeans. She still wears high-end, amazing business suits, but the relationship we have has spanned more than twenty years and I am so grateful to have her in my life.

"Mandi is like an exploding soda: when she sees you she's delighted. It's as if she hasn't seen you in years. She doesn't let rules define her which makes her interesting. She's like a favorite pair of leggings, your

go-to, the thing you can't wait to be with. She's like an awesome toddler: She's curious. She Digs in. She's constantly asking questions and wants to know more about the person she's interacting with."

Shawna Bumpus, Senior Vice President, Morgan Stanley.

Once you've built the relationship and get a customer to talk to you, then what? So much can happen in this phase of the process. The client can be interested, and then go dark. The client can get your proposal and then lag on making a decision. It's important to look for creative and unique ways to stay in front of the customer, building that relationship, even if you're not in an active sales cycle with that person. When a customer goes cold on you, here is a tactic I've used over the years that always works for me.

sales tale:

A "CHOOSE YOUR OWN ADVENTURE EMAIL" WILL GET COLD CUSTOMERS TO RESPOND

You finally have some good leads. Good for you! But sometimes good leads turn into dead leads. Sometimes you start with spectacular email banter, but then... where oh where did they go? When they go COLD on you—and I mean COLD—like crickets, totally silent after multiple emails and phone calls, it leaves you wondering what the heck to do? Some people may quit at this point assuming the client isn't interested. Don't do it. Don't be the 80% of people who quit when someone goes cold on you. This is the part where the real fun begins. This is an opportunity to develop a deeper relationship with the client. You have no idea what is happening on their end. Maybe they changed jobs? Maybe they are so busy they can't even think of inviting a new vendor into their world? Maybe their dog is sick, or they got sick, or they hate their boss, or they won the lottery? You just don't know and the only way to know is to ask. One day back in 2006, my brother in-law and I were talking about how to get people to call us back. He was telling me about this amazing email he used on a customer that got an instant response. He called it the "Choose Your Own Adventure" email. I took the concept, put a little spin of my own on it, and below is the result. I've been using this for years and its return rate is huge. There are maybe just two times (in all the many times I've used this tactic) where I didn't receive a response. All the other times I've sent a Choose Your Own Adventure email, I've had an instant response. The response isn't always favorable. Sometimes the response is, "I am not using your service anymore." This is the worst-case scenario, however, a response is a response. And, a response—good or bad opens the door to other conversations.

The important thing about this email is you have to know a little bit about the customer. You can investigate this on Facebook, Instagram, LinkedIn, or even refer to notes from previous conversations. In this circumstance, I knew the client went to UNC Chapel Hill, loves BBQ sauce, and is a mom with a couple of kids. I knew this from a couple of previous conversations, coupled with her LinkedIn profile. Here's an example:

Client (name hidden to protect the innocent),

Happy Tuesday, how are you? I haven't heard from you in a while and assume you're on an adventure.

Are you:

1. Rallying up the UNC Alumnae for some March Madness watch parties?
2. Taste testing a bevy of BBQ Sauce in prep for summer BBQ season?
3. Juggling spring break family scheduling?
4. None of the above, just slammed with work and life, have been thinking about my proposal but haven't had time to get back to me yet?

Whichever adventure you've been on, will you let me know when you catch a moment? I am cool with whatever's been happening in your world—just want to get a pulse check to know whether I should keep bugging you OR leave you alone to live your adventures :)

Thanks again for considering working with me. Would love to work together. Have a great day.

END AMAZING EXAMPLE....

I shared this email template with a couple of sales coaching clients recently and they took it to a new level. They created an infographic. It got an instant response. Take this and use it, my brother in-law and I don't mind. If it helps you get a response from a client, we salute and endorse the use of this strange, risky—yet fun—email.

The gist of this is that you have to have a voice and a personality. You have to constantly be trying different ways to communicate with customers. Email inboxes are flooded. No one answers the phone or checks voicemails. Customers are doing ten jobs, wearing twenty hats but getting paid for one job. Life is busy and stressful. You must find a way to be a break in the day for a potential customer and give them a reason to want to talk to you—even if it's just because you made them laugh or took them down memory lane.

sales tale:
DO THINGS YOU LOVE WITH CUSTOMERS TO BUILD BETTER RELATIONSHIPS

I was on a sales trip in Arizona many years ago when a client and I were chatting about her intramural volleyball league. She happened to need a girl to sub in that night. It happened that I didn't have dinner plans that night because my other client cancelled due to a sick kid at home. It was kismet. She asked if I'd be interested in subbing in on the team and I said yes. I am not good at volleyball—at all. In fact, there is some lore about a beach volleyball team I joined in San Diego in the early 2000s where I was so bad that one time, I caught the ball. Needless to say, I was not invited back on that team. This time I knew I had to be at my best, which meant, *do not catch the damn ball*. I met my client and her teammates at the court, and we played. It was super fun. Half were hotel people—competitors of mine—and the other half weren't in the hospitality industry. We played for a couple hours, got a nice workout in, and we won! We shared a victory and a volleyball court together. Most importantly, we shared memories. She got to know me on a different level—she got to see my competitive spirit and good sportsmanship. I got to see her interact with other hotel people, which served as a model for our future interactions. Overall, it was a win-win and we did a couple deals together after that night. Our interactions while negotiating the contract for those deals were much more amicable. She was a fair customer but knew exactly what she needed. I was a fair negotiator, but it was much less adversarial because we now had a relationship that went deeper than a lame lunch at Del Friscos.

I love spin class. I especially love doing spin when I am on the road. It's fun to find a spin studio near the hotel and take a spin class early in the morning before the day's mayhem ensues. I started doing this several years ago and now whenever I travel for work, I collect people to join me. I have one vendor/friend who I can always rely on to spin with me when I travel. Together, we rally clients, peers, and other vendors to spin with us at the local SoulCycle or CycleBar. We meet, we spin, we sweat and then grab a coffee or juice together after. Guess what? With that one partner, I booked two million dollars in business, in just one year—that same year we started spinning together. Something we discovered during one of our conversations is that we both love Howard Stern interviews. We still text about the good ones—Eddie Vedder, Tom Brady, Hillary Clinton. During the pandemic when my client had to cancel her meeting and move it to another year, we worked through that amicably. I have had many not-so-amicable moments with my hotel partners during Covid-19. However, since there was an established relationship in place, we were able to work through it in a reasonable way that worked for the hotel and the client. It all started with a love of spin and some good chats about Howard. It's evolved into a great friendship and an awesome business relationship. When I have a program that might fit the profile of his hotel he's my first call. I know spin isn't for everyone. The point is to find more creative ways to engage with your customers—and to save yourself from stale pork sliders. Do you like to read? Start a business book club. I've been in those before. Do you like to dance? Create a dance-off or dance party with some clients. Find common ground in a unique way that is fun for you and the client to cement the relationship for life.

THE VOICE OF THE CUSTOMER—AN EXERCISE

If you think you know your customer, you probably don't. Their business changes, their voices change. You can't stop getting to know a customer just because you've been working together for a long time. Just like every relationship, you have to water it, grow it and continue to get to know each other.

I delivered a coaching session to a sales team in 2019. The premise was to continue building relationships with your customers by understanding their voice. It's really important to listen to the voice of the customer. It's equally important to understand that your customer's voice may change over time and to be connected to that change. I did a coaching session with a group of twenty salespeople and below is an excerpt of the coaching session. In preparation for the coaching session, I surveyed some customers and asked them 3 questions:

1. What makes a good vendor?
2. What makes a bad vendor?
3. What keeps you up at night about your job?

My clients weren't that surprised about the questions because I ask them these questions when I first start working with them. However, in asking them these questions, I realized that their answers were much different today than they were when we started working together. Their voices had changed. Their businesses had changed. Their needs had changed. This was a good reminder for me to keep asking my customers these questions. These types of questions are the keys to the kingdom. A customer is telling you what they want, what they don't want and what is worrying them. All you have to do is listen and take action. This removes the secrets and the uncertainty about what it will take to earn their business. They are telling you—and you can use the information to not only earn their business but to establish value and keep earning it repeatedly. Here are the results of the mini focus group:

WHAT MAKES A GOOD VENDOR?

- Listens
- Someone that "gets me"
- Quality customer service
- Knows that I am a non-profit and on a budget. I don't expect free, but do expect fair
- Someone that treats me and their vendor counterparts the way I treat them—with respect
- Reliability/Trust
- Communication
- Be of Service
- Always adding value, knows the business

BELOW ARE EXACT WORDS FROM THE CLIENTS SURVEYED:

Customer Voice:"A good vendor listens, not the kind of listening that requires one to say nothing until it's your turn to speak but the kind that hears beyond the conversation."

Let's chew on that for a minute—can you think of an example of a time when you listened to a customer so hard that you heard beyond the conversation and delivered stellar service?

Customer Voice: "A good vendor is someone who is consistent with response times, openly and promptly shares challenges, and follows up after the service."

Can you think of a situation where your response time or follow-through helped you secure the business or keep the business?

NOW, ONTO THE BAD VENDORS. WHAT MAKES A BAD VENDOR?

- Makes my job harder
- Pushing their own agenda
- Inconsistency—great job one time and then bad job another time
- Not listening
- Sales robot
- If a mistake happens, they don't apologize or do anything to recover
- Unforeseen fees not disclosed
- Someone who is rude to other vendors, my team, presenters
- No follow-through
- Bad communication

Customer Voice: "If a vendor does something to break my trust, I will never work with that company again. I usually send a strongly worded letter to them and cc their supervisor or CEO."

That's pretty intense right? These people are so busy but they are OK with making time to send a nasty gram? It's because service matters to them.

> **Customer Voice:** "I don't want to do the math if you're supposed to do the math. Don't make me do math."

This is funny but you would be shocked how frequently I see this. People submitting proposals and contracts to me where the numbers don't add up, where the percentages and dates are wrong, or where they make me pull from three different emails to get one answer. Whatever you can do to make your clients' job easier, DO IT, DO IT, DO IT.

Can you think of a time where you turned a client around after they had a bad experience with someone in your industry that did the exact same thing? How can you build on that for all your customers?

AND, WHAT KEEPS YOU UP AT NIGHT ABOUT YOUR JOB?

- Hoping all the pieces and moving parts pull together
- Finding new ways to keep internal customers happy
- Building on being better than last year
- Something not going as planned because of poor communication

> **Customer Voice:** "I want to know the good and the bad. I wrap honesty in with communication. Tell me the real deal and I can figure out how to make it work but I want to know."

Below is an activity I did with the group. I encourage you to do this in your work team, or even your family.

A QUICK ACTIVITY

In my house growing up we had a plethora of index cards. My mom used them to make her grocery list. My dad carried them around in his front pocket—and still does, with random projects around the house listed. To this day, I still have index cards pinned to the bulletin board in my office. Now that we've talked about the voice of the customer, grab yourself an index card and let's put it into practice.

What are three actions you can take in the next six months that help you be a good vendor? Think about what you're currently doing and the voice of the customer—is there anything else you can do? Write them down on an index card and post them in your office.

Share them with me at coach@mandigraziano.com, I want to see them. If you email them to me and the date you want them done, I will follow up with you along the way to see if you're on track.

Our voice isn't always our customer's voice. Doing this exercise is a great reminder to be asking customers the same questions over the years. Their minds may change, their business may change. Whichever the case, understanding the voice of your customer is an awesome way to be the most valuable vendor you can possibly be.

STAY IN TOUCH AND DON'T BURN BRIDGES

I collect people. Some people like that about me. Some people run like the wind when they hear from me. I have no fear about either scenario. If you meet someone you like, or connect with in a business or personal setting, stay in touch. You don't have to be best friends. You can be LinkedIn buddies or occasional networking friends. If you connect with that person, stay in touch. Sometimes I will connect with a vendor I have no intention of buying from but I like their personality. I will stay in touch with them the same way I will stay in touch with a client or a college gal pal. I believe surrounding yourself with good people is good for the soul. You never know if, in the future, you can give that person a job or they can give you one. You never know if that person will introduce you to the love of your life or your future divorce attorney. I've stayed in touch with people I enjoy from every job I've had. As a result, I have never had to go "looking" for a job in twenty years. Ever since my first hotel job in San Diego, all of my job hunting has been done by word of mouth—through past co-workers or clients. Most of the sales and business coaching and speaking gigs I do are with people I have known over the years or referrals from those people. You have to stay in touch and stay on people's radars.

SWEATworking. This is a mix of clients and vendors before a long day of conferences and after a very sweaty six-thirty in the morning SoulCycle class

Client visits don't have to be boring, rent a BIRD and fly around town to see hotels. You don't need a stuffy car service or UBER black. Enjoy the fresh air and have an experience with your customers—and her mom!

Clients and vendors SWEATworking, friends and business partners. We get stuff done.

CHAPTER FOUR

don't be a vanna—the privilege of presentation

When you earn a moment to interact with a customer, you have to put everything you have into each meeting, appointment, agenda and presentation. When someone says yes, don't take it lightly. Be creative, be present, be thankful.

- Mandi-ism

Pitching to a client, making a presentation, or visually sharing your story is a privilege. If you are lucky enough to make it to this point in the sales process, you can't take it lightly. It's important to me to always create a custom presentation. Canned, boring templates just won't do. I am sure there is an efficiency expert out there who hates what I am saying about customization. It's also important to me to make every face-to-face or face-to-phone experience memorable. The more customized the experience, the better. However, each business scenario is different. Each client is different. Each need and circumstance leading into that presentation is different. The more you can show that you've listened to the client along the way and that you truly understand their problem, the better the presentation will be. I am a big fan of creativity, and an equally big fan of the facts. Data does not lie. Before your first meeting or phone call, the client may not like you or may not be ready to trust you. One solid way to establish trust is through your presentation. Show them you've thought about the presentation, their business, their needs and them personally and you'll have a client for life.

Every opportunity to be face-to-face or face-to-virtual with a customer is a presentation. I look at sales meetings as a presentation. I look at a quick catch-up call as a presentation. Time is valuable and you have to leave your client or potential customer with a takeaway each time.

Before each presentation I have a set of rules I apply:

Rule #1: Practice, practice, practice. I like to know how much time I have. I write out every single word I am going to say and then read it out loud three times. I insert pauses where I want to make a point, get a laugh, or where I think there will be questions. I actually write the word *pause* on my script.

Rule #2: Do a run-through with a friend or family member. Kids are perfect for this because they are honest and will ask questions. You want to practice getting stumped by questions. You want to practice how your voice sounds. It often sounds better in writing than it does out loud so you need to give yourself time to perfect your presentation style.

Rule #3: Look at yourself in the mirror. You may think your smile is charming, until you see it in your wedding pictures and every photo looks like you are growling at your husband. For a business setting, it helps to know what you look like when you are speaking. You may need to calm down the eyebrows or hand gestures if it feels scary to yourself in the mirror. I have a mirror next to my desk so when I am talking on the phone I can see if I am smiling. It's more pleasant to talk to people who are smiling than people who are worried about what they are going to say next.

Since so much of what we do is remote these days, I am ready for a presentation in a moment's notice. In my home office I have a beauty drawer. It has red lipstick, a mirror and a brush. That way, if someone wants to hop on a quick virtual call, I am ready and look semi presentable even if I am in my gym clothes from the waist down.

Rule #4: Know the medium you are using in advance. Know the equipment the client is using before you travel to the meeting so you can be sure everything is compatible and make any last-minute adjustments. Arrive early to set up and run through your presentation. Sometimes I will even drive from my hotel to the presentation location the night before just so I know exactly how much time it takes because the GPS can lie.

Ask the customer what the dress code is for the company and then dress up a little more. Unless your brand relies on your outfit, it's better to be slightly overdressed than underdressed.

Rule #5: Plan to leave the client with something. It doesn't have to be big or expensive. It should be creative and relevant to your product or service. If you are doing a virtual presentation, you can email the client links to gifts before or after. In the past where I've done presentations in person and a portion of the team was dialing in for the call, I would send a Starbucks gift card in advance. That way the people at home can have a cup of coffee with me and the others in person during the presentation. If you want to do something less cliché, donate to the client's favorite charity, or get a gift card from a specialty online shopping site like The W Marketplace, Sugarwish, or Stitch Fix.

Rule #6: Numbers don't lie but they can be boring. I am a big fan of numbers and stats in presentations. However, I am NOT a big fan of being bored. Try to create one slide showing how the numbers will improve business productivity, or make the business more money. It's so important to have factual data, but you have to balance it with keeping your audience interested. Pick the top five stats that matter to the client. (You should know this because you've asked open-ended questions in advance of the appointment.) Sometimes you don't know this from their answers but from the research you've done in advance. *Don't tell me about you. Tell me about me. What's in it for me?* Numbers are not emotional and they can help with faster decisions when there's something in it for the client.

Rule #7: Know your competition and how to sell against them.

An in-person or virtual presentation is the perfect time to sell against your competition. Before the meeting, make a list of what you know about yourself and your competition. Make a list of the strengths you have over your competition. Make a list of the areas where you're equal. Make a list of your weaknesses. Do not speak in a negative way about the competition—I have seen that many times and it's a turn off. You can, however, highlight why you're better than your competition. You don't even have to say your competitor's name. You can simply say, "One of the main reasons people love using our firm is because we only assign one person to the account and that one person will see you through from start to finish. We do not have an account manager start with you and then turn you over to three different people." In this circumstance, you know that your competitor has a front-facing account manager who then turns it over to a team of people. Before a presentation, I like to make a grid of why we are better than the competition so if it comes up I can speak to it without trash-talking anyone.

sales tale:

A SPARK OF INSPIRATION, THIS WAY

One warm yet breezy evening in San Diego back in 2011, I was wandering the streets of a cute community event called The WalkAbout. The artsy merchants of the neighborhood open their doors once a month to allow residents to walk through the various shops, eateries, and galleries to sample the wares and talk to the owners.

As I wandered the streets, at the base of a very dark side alley sat a cardboard sign on an easel that said, "Spark Of Inspiration, This Way..." with an arrow in votive candles pointing down the dark alley. I was intrigued so I followed the sign. The alley was lined with small votive candles that led me to a garage. The garage was filled with vibrant, colorful art and was clearly the home studio of a local artist. I perused her paintings of elephants, robots, and abstract faces and struck up a conversation with the artist. She was personable, crafty and a smart marketer. I loved her creativity so much that I hired her to create the logo for my coaching business. She didn't have a storefront at the Walkabout. She didn't even have a working gallery at that time. She just had an idea, and a hook to create enough intrigue to get people— well, at least one—to walk down that dark alley to see her creations. I've purchased several pieces of art from her over the years and we commissioned a piece for our wedding. Our living room wall now wears a one-of-a-kind robot wedding piece she created just for us. That alley artist now has a fancy gallery in New Mexico and I can barely afford her work so I am glad we met her when we did. We never would have met her if she didn't put some creativity into how she was presenting herself and her business. I never would have had a company logo—at least not one as cool as the one she created for me—had I not walked down that alley. Making presentations and being creative can take time but can return on your investment tenfold.

sales tale:
KILLER SITE INSPECTIONS

In the hotel business, we do site inspections. Site inspections are a presentation to potential clients to showcase the hotel, city or convention center. It's an opportunity to learn more about the customer and get to know their needs. I encourage you to make it personal, be as creative as possible and know everything you can about the client before the presentation.

I once did a site inspection for a building that wasn't even built. It was a sales meeting for a growing medical company. We went online and researched the main decision maker, the VP of Sales. He, like most people in a VP of Sales role, had a lot of energy and wanted the meeting to be high energy with a theme that excited the audience. Since we only had a raw building that was under construction, we had our work cut out for us. We invited him and his team to our "pre-sales office." We gave all of them custom hard hats with our logo—which was a rockstar tattoo. In advance we had asked them to tell us the first first concert they attended. We created name tags that were styled like backstage passes, that had the first concert they went to listed. We fed them. We played six songs from their first concerts on a loop in the video when they arrived and departed. After the quick presentation in the sales office, we took them to the building, which was under construction and gave them a backstage tour. We used words like "Imagine" (John Lennon) and "Picture This" (J Giles) so the music theme ran through the presentation. At the end of the site inspection we asked the VP of Sales, "Can you *imagine* your sales team getting revved up about your business in this building?" He said, "YES. This is the most fun I've ever had on a site inspection!" And we booked it. It was an awesome meeting, and we didn't even have a building to sell at that time. However, we gave him the "feels" that his attendees would have and created a vision. We solved his problem of "theme" and "getting salespeople excited to sell their product." We did it for him. Selling an unfinished product or building can be tricky. Using keywords like "imagine" in the process opened their minds to creativity. He even gave us some new ideas. In this circumstance the customer was buying confidence as our product was not complete. It's important to present confidence and creativity when a building or product is not complete but you're trying to get investor and customer buy in.

sales tale:
MAKE IT PERSONAL

I was at the peak of my health kick. I was riding my bike everywhere as a bike commuter and walking everywhere I could. I was the healthiest I'd ever been, and I shined, girl, I shined. It was no surprise that the universe delivered me a conference opportunity that needed a home. It was an active, healthy living association. I researched the founder and realized he was a man obsessed with walking and consulted for developers to create walking paths in new housing communities. We greeted the client wearing bright white tennis shoes. We took the stairs for every single level and put footprint decals on the floor of the building to outline a walking path. We had "Walk This Way" by Aerosmith playing and took pictures with him in front of the Abbey Road Mural where the Beatles were "walking in the background." Our follow-up kept the same branding continuity with the "Walk This Way" picture of him on the follow-up proposal. We won the business, because we took a little extra time to get out of our boring hotel suit and heels and spoke his language. BONUS: I probably burned 1500 calories on the site inspection.

sales tale:
UNLEASH YOUR CREATIVITY

I went to a site inspection as a client a couple years ago in Jacksonville, Florida. This hotel did everything to make it personal. I was scouting a potential venue for a conference related to the barbecue industry. When I arrived at the hotel at nine that night they had the logo of the association lit up behind the front desk and on the floor. When I went into my guest room they had another logo imprinted on the pillow cases. They also had a couple pictures of my husband and I and our dog in frames on the desk. The note said, "You spend so much time on the road, we wanted to bring your family to you." It was really nice to be welcomed that way after a long day of traveling. The next morning we had breakfast and did a site inspection. During breakfast, an intern dressed as a pig greeted me. I didn't quite get it at first but thought it was cute. After breakfast as we walked the space and rounded the corner, there was that pig again. This time, the pig was being chased by someone in a chef's costume with BBQ tongs. It was hilarious. Throughout the visit, the pig and chef would show up and aside from making me laugh, I appreciated the clever way they kept their hotel in the front of my mind in the selection process. After the visit, we sat down in a meeting room with red and white checkered tablecloths where the entire team walked in wearing chef's hats and aprons. They had made custom aprons for me and my clients. This was a hotel that wanted the business and we booked them. The meeting space and location worked really well and so many other elements were perfect. However, the creativity in the presentation was what put it over the top.

TIPS AND TRICKS FOR VIRTUAL PRESENTATIONS

In the age of Covid-19 we all learned how to be masters at the virtual presentation. This brought a new set of challenges, as well as opportunities to be creative. The biggest thing to remember about a virtual presentation is that you might only get one shot at the sale. Prior to Covid-19 it might have been a prelude to an in-person meeting but post-pandemic, one video chat might be all you get. I need to know everything you need me to know in order to make a decision as soon as I get off the phone. You may not get another chance so make it good, memorable, statistically relevant and leave me wanting more. The presentation should never be more than forty-five minutes.

WEAR EARBUDS OR HEADPHONES

Background noise is loud and intrusive. It's good for both parties to be wearing earbuds or headphones. This way each side can hear all questions and answers and block out all forms of additional noise. Consider sending the client some branded earbuds in advance to make your presentation that much more noteworthy.

THE "ROVING REPORTER" TECHNIQUE

I love this technique when you have a product or service with a lot of moving parts. Treat it like a live news broadcast to keep people interested and ensure that you don't waste time with transitions. For example, if you are selling real estate, "throw" us to different parts of the property as the salesperson walks from space to space. We don't want to see you walk. Cue each person in each part of the project and then "throw it back" to the salesperson.

HAVE A DEDICATED CAMERA PERSON AND EMCEE

One hotel did an awesome job at having one person own the call. He served as the emcee. Although he wasn't on the property, he guided us through the site while the camera person showed us what the salesperson was explaining. I've been on a couple virtual site inspections where the salesperson is explaining something and the camera person is pointing the device at something completely different to what is being explained. Another hotel had an equal counterpart holding the device, while the salesperson did the tour. I appreciated the product knowledge the camera person had about the property for two reasons. First, the person holding the camera was able to quickly answer questions while the other person was walking to the next spot on the tour. And second, the person holding the camera understood what the salesperson was explaining so he panned to all the right visual elements to match the descriptions.

DON'T BE A VANNA

Don't get me wrong, I love Vanna White. (I actually met her when I did a summer internship for a production company where she filmed the <u>Easy Glider Infomercial</u>. She was a nice lady.) What I mean by "Don't Be A Vanna" is *don't just turn the letters*. We are now doing virtual presentations to gather an abundance of decision-making information at one time. We have to hang up the call and have enough information to decide. We rely on the salesperson to be more than the person holding their hand out waving at us. Use stories to tell me how your product or service is superior. I want to hear specific examples of how you can make my life better. When a salesperson is just *"turning the letters"* it's not the best use of anyone's time.

USE A RELIABLE PLATFORM AND DEVICE

Everyone's device is different and reacts differently to presentation and meeting platforms. We all have our technology limitations. Figure out what is best for you and suggest using that medium for the call. Be sure to talk about it before the virtual site tour so everyone on both sides is on the same page. Virtual presentations will drain your device's battery so be ready with a backup. Or give the presentation with the device plugged in if you're able to stay stationary. Make time before the call to test your device so you know how long it can last using that exact medium.

INVOLVE PEOPLE WHO ADD VALUE

Most clients want to hear from the owner, founder or general manager. Clients want to hear how the company started and the company's plan to stay relevant—especially if this is an investor pitch. They want to hear from the top brass how they helped other clients, just like them, with specific examples. Even if it's a quick cameo, that personal interaction with the owner or manager is meaningful. Be sure to give that person talking points so they don't bogart the whole presentation. Having more than two people on the camera in the same shot at one time gets confusing and can be hard to hear. Try to limit it to one or two people making a cameo at the same time.

Tim's Tale of Mandi's Awkward-Yet-Memorable Presentation:

"I took a chance on hiring Mandi for an extremely competitive role, based nearly entirely on the slightly audacious, fun, and creative "Mandi Notebook" she sent across the country to me back in 2000. She blew me away with her energy, creativity, and originality. If ever there was a master at making memorable and interesting presentations, Mandi is the real deal."

Tim Mulligan, JD, Chief Human Resources Officer | Allen Institute for AI (AI2) | Author | Playwright.

Tim is being nice. My notebook was awful. (See end of the chapter.) However, the important thing to remember is that it was different from anything he had seen. Although it was bad, it was memorable. I didn't have any experience, but he hired me anyway because of the time I took to be creative and the energetic way in which I presented myself. If Tim had not hired me, I'm not sure what direction my career would have taken. I am so grateful that he took a chance on a young, inexperienced salesperson and had the vision to see through my odd-yet-creative Mandi book. My career in hospitality took off because of him and I am forever grateful. Tim is one of the most talented people I know. He writes books, screenplays, and cookbooks all while managing a successful and demanding career. Oh and he is a dad to two young adults and a partner, all at the same time. He is creative and hilarious so to get a compliment from him about creativity is an honor. I've seen him make presentations over the years about sensitive topics such as sexual harassment, workplace injuries, and developing leaders. His presentations are always loaded with facts and solid information. However, his delivery is what gets you. He keeps audiences engaged with his humor and no-nonsense style. I am grateful to have watched him in action over the years and to call him a friend.

RESUMES

Your resume is a form of a presentation. This might be the first thing people see about you and decide if they want to see more. Over the years I have created interesting resumes to capture the attention of the interviewer. I have helped countless people with their resumes to ensure my friends, family and clients better present themselves for a potential job. I am not a human resource professional and can't speak to it from that perspective. I can say, of the resumes I have done, I've always gotten the job. Even when my resume was awful, the time and creativity that was taken to create the resume helped keep me in the conversation. When I wanted a job at a music branded hotel, I looked at their website, looked at their color choices and the words they used to describe their brand. Irreverent, Rockstar and A-list were all words they used through their website so I incorporated them into my resume. Instead of Job Experience I used Irreverent Experience. Instead of Qualifications I used Rockstar Skills. Instead of Organizations I used A-List Affiliations. I knew the hotel was very focused on food and beverage so I sliced the resume down in size and made it slimmer and thicker, like an actual menu.

I once interviewed with a man who was a professor. He had mentioned in some previous conversations how much he loves overhead projectors even though we were in the PowerPoint era. I printed my resume on clear plastic overhead projector paper so when he looked at it he could pop it on his favorite medium and look at it on the big screen. When you're writing a resume, use a thesaurus and use action words. If the job you're going for is in medical, lead with your medical experience. It's OK if it's mentioned in the cover and it's not in chronological order—don't bury the lead. Put the body of the email in chronological order. Be brief, be bright and be gone. Be sure to present yourself in a memorable way. My first resume for the hotel business was a "Mandi Book"—it was awful. It was a binder with the portfolio of events I had done and marketing pieces I had created along with testimonials and letters of recommendations. The front page was a picture of a girl yelling, it felt like me.

My experience was not vast. I was only twenty-four years old. But, there was personality behind it and the crazy girl picture on the front made me memorable. Don't be afraid to be unique and be you when presenting yourself in the resume process. Be sure to do your research on the type of company and incorporate some of their messages and culture words into your resume if it's a good fit.

INTERNAL MEETINGS

Internal meetings with peers, bosses and subordinates are also a form of presentation. This is a high-power time to instill confidence in other meeting goers. I have a rule with coaching clients that I always have an agenda for each meeting and I send that agenda twenty four hours prior to the meeting. This way, people can mentally prepare for the meeting and the meeting can be productive. The meeting agenda should follow the same format each week as creating consistency creates momentum and cohesiveness within a team. It also helps people feel comfortable and know what to expect so they are more likely to participate and be better contributors to the meeting. Below is a sample meeting agenda.

SAMPLE MEETING AGENDA

- **Positive Focus:** (round the room, 1 positive thing)
- **Top Sales from previous week:** (top 3) how did they do it? (praise the top and have them share story)
- **What's On Tap:** (round the room by department or individual—one top priority for the upcoming week, how they will tackle)
- **Sales Tip of the Week:** (pick something relevant, give examples/stories, ask how it has or can be applied to current open business)
- **What Keeps You Up at Night?** (opportunity for anyone to ask for help if need it)
- **Wrap Up:** (close with a quote or an action step or take away)

MEETINGS DON'T HAVE TO SUCK

Stay positive. Encourage laughter. Let the good vibes flow through the meeting and allow the energy to stay upbeat. During Covid-19 instead of asking, "How are you today?" I asked, "What's something that made you laugh this week?" At that time, we all knew that everyone was stressed, bored, busy, pivoting, trying not to lay people off, trying not to gain the Covid-15, homeschooling kids, taking the dog on endless walks, spending more money than ever before at the grocery store and hoarding flour and face masks. Differentiate yourself by asking, "What made you laugh today?" People want to participate in meetings, contribute and feel significant. They don't want to be talked at, or lectured. Find ways to encourage contribution and collaboration in your meetings. Your next big idea could be from the intern or the baby boomer, but it's up to you to facilitate an environment where everyone feels comfortable contributing.

REVMAX

When I worked for hotels, we had two standing daily meetings. We had a "RevMax" meeting which was short for "Revenue Maximization." At RevMax, we sat around a board table with our sales team. Each salesperson had to pitch the business they wanted to sell that day to each other. As a team we would vote if we'd take the business or not. The voting was based on the RevMax Five: History, Rate, Competition, Food/Beverage and Meeting Space. At the beginning of my hotel sales career I was gobbled up at this table. I would lose day after day. I saw senior people getting rejected too but was determined to crack the case on how to get these internal people to say yes.

Once I realized that I needed to do my research, come prepared, be confident with my pitch, and present why this was a good fit for the hotel, then, I was unstoppable. At that table a salesperson had to appeal to her peers, her boss and the revenue director. Each person in the audience had a different motivation. The boss and revenue director wanted the most business on the books and wanted to layer business in to maximize rate. Peers each had their own business to pitch and sometimes your business was competing for dates so yours had to be better. The key to victory in these meetings was to know what the client paid in the past. I had to research website registrations or just ask the client. It helped to know who else they were looking at, the food and beverage budget and what meeting space they needed.

All these factors go into the "RevMax Five" and if you went to the table with the RevMax four or the RevMax three, you'd likely get turned down. Every single lead I brought into that room, I had my RevMax Five, and sometimes I had RevMax six or seven, but never less than five. I presented with confidence, was prepared with visual aids and was relentless about getting my business approved. I'd bring the same piece of business back again and again until it was approved. Each time I'd present a different set of dates, or ask the customer if they could modify something about their program to make it more attractive—or since salespeople have short memories, and if the conference was many years out, I'd wait a week, take the temperature of the room and bring it back. This was a daily internal meeting that, with practice, I got really good at and learned a valuable lesson about confidence in internal meetings.

Mandi Kobasic   mkobasic@msn.com

Authentic Skills
Multi-Year Contract Negotiation Knowledge, Prospecting skills using LinkedIn, Hoovers, Knowland Group, Social Media Tools, Perception selling and overcoming objections with down economy, "AIG & Wells Fargo Effect", Sales leadership in teams and cross selling multi products.

Diamond Meeting Experience
Hard Rock Hotel San Diego, Account Director, February 2007 - current
420 rooms, 40,000 square feet meeting space
Books groups of 101 rooms peak and above, West Coast (California, Washington, Oregon, Canada, Texas, Colorado, Utah, Arizona)
Manages strategic prospecting efforts for west coast sales team--West Coast Posse
Cloned West Coast Posse Strategic Account Management team at San Mateo Marriott-a Tarsadia Hotel. Facilitated Implementation
Regular Presentations to Top Accounts West Coast--CISCO, MICROSOFT, ALLERGAN, HPN, AMYLIN, SONY and QUALCOMM
Obtained 113% sales goal 2008 and booked $1.5 million in 2009.
West Coast team-111% Jan. 2010 goal.
Awards: Sales Person of the Year: 2008, Tarsadia Hotels

EnDev LLC, Director of Sales Stingaree, Side Bar & The Witherby, September 2005 – January 2007
EnDev LLC is a San Diego Headquartered company which specializes in operating restaurants, nightclubs and private event venues along with development of land for mixed-use businesses.
Lead sales efforts for all venues inside the EnDev portfolio with main focus on event sales
Opened Stingaree in December 2005, Opened The Witherby in December 2006
Set prices and sales strategy for new venues in pre sell phase
Hire, manage, train and develop sales team• Created Hotel Partner Program as a lead source
Analyzed reports, pace, forecast, P/L, and reported to investors quarterly
Created investor business referral program
Negotiate and buy advertising for meetings and convention media
Obtained 200% of sales goals for event sales, and over 100% for venues overall

Sheraton San Diego Hotel & Marina, National Sales Manager, August 2003 - August 2005
Sold 1,044 guest room hotel, 90,000 square feet-meeting space- multiple markets
Negotiate contracts, prospect for new business, build existing accounts and sell value
Train/develop small meetings managers & sales coordinators to meet their career objectives.
Obtained 162% of 2004 Sales Goal, Obtained 102% of 2005 Sales Goal by August
Awards: 2004 Sales Person of the Year-Starwood Hotels & Resorts Worldwide, West Coast and 2005 Top Producer, West Coast Region

Sheraton San Diego Hotel & Marina, Catering Sales Manager September 2000 - August 2003
Sold and Managed events for 10 - 1,000 guests
Upsell existing contracts, customized menus, work with banquet staff in event coordination
Built local corporate market post September 11th to $1 million market in 1 year
Prospected for new clients and built local corporate market base
Obtained 131% of 2001 sales goal, 115% of 2002 sales goal, 120% of 2003 sales goal by August

Michaud's Town N Country, Cleveland-Ohio, Marketing Manager, March 1, 1998 - July 2000
45, 000 square foot banquet & conference center
Trained event sales staff of 4 to sell and service special events of 10 - 800 guests
Grew midweek corporate business 30% in the first 6 months
Media Buying (broadcasting, print and electronic media), Cross sold area hotels.
Created, Designed and Published all Marketing Collateral, Built web site, managed online marketing

My transparency paper resume for the Professor-like hiring manager.

Rockstar Red Resume when I interviewed for Hard Rock
Hotels sales job

The "somewhat audacious" Mandi Book that landed me the job with
Tim Mulligan.

Logo that was created from the artist I found in the dark alley who compelled me to find her with her Spark of Inspiration sign.

Robot art given to us as a wedding gift from the local artist we found in the alley from her Spark of Inspiration sign.

CHAPTER FIVE

time is your greatest asset

Time is your greatest asset, use it wisely. Who you spend your time with and how you spend your time is important. Pay attention. - Mandi-ism

The biggest error I see businesses make is the way each salesperson, business owner or employee manages their time. I see it all the time when I coach clients. I see it all the time as a client too. I've personally made the mistake myself over the years. Time is our greatest asset. How we use our time can make or break us financially. Time really is money and should be treated as such. I know it is cliché but it's the truth and is the biggest difference between successful and unsuccessful people. Don't waste time with internet rabbit holes, bad clients, mean people, gossip, or stuff you can't afford that doesn't move your life forward. Using your time wisely will create balance. Abusing your time will create distress. We have more time than we realize and when we take the time to understand exactly how we're using our time, we are powerful.

HOW A NEAR-DEATH EXPERIENCE TAUGHT ME THE VALUE OF TIME MANAGEMENT

Two weeks before our wedding my fiancé and I had just picked up his wedding suit and my rehearsal dress. We were sitting in his car in the parking lot after a delicious and relaxing lunch on a sunny San Diego patio. We were planning our weekend, AKA we were fighting about our plans for the weekend. He wanted to watch World Cup Soccer matches with his pals. I wanted to do a hike with my gal pals. However, there was still a list of wedding chores to be done. I can't remember the task, but it was time sensitive and needed to be done the next morning. One of us was going to have to sacrifice our personal friend time to do the wedding task. We were both holding our ground as if it were a duel with both our guns drawn. Neither one of us was giving up. It was a standard, stupid, pre wedding argument to which someone always ends up giving up what they want to do most. Despite the argument, everything for the wedding was coming together and I was so excited to be getting married to my buddy in a couple of weeks.

My fiancé was in the driver's seat getting ready to turn the car on when he started coughing really hard, as if he had super thick loogies in his throat. (I was annoyed because he does this. He exaggerates his cough and relishes in every moment of snot he can conjure up for every sniff and cough. Every morning he does this for at least ten minutes and I call it

"The Scooter Symphony.") The Scooter Symphony this time sounded much more dramatic and elaborate. He coughed again—this time hanging his head out the window. There was a loud rattling accompanying the cough that sounded hollow and like something was stuck. He started choking on his own blood. It was the reddest blood I had ever seen in my whole life. He rolled out of the driver's seat onto the ground and choked again. I got out of the car, guided him to the passenger side and hopped in the driver's seat. I was driving him to the hospital. I got to the exit of the parking lot to turn onto the street and he started coughing again. He jumped out of the car, sat on the curb in the parking lot, put his head in his hands, and more blood was coming out of his mouth. I dialed 911 and within minutes an ambulance arrived. I looked over at my fiancé. A staff member from the restaurant where we had just eaten had given him a white towel to clean up the blood that was on his face, mouth, and teeth. My fiancé was pensively looking into the air. He was calm and looked at peace. I would later learn he was looking at light—calm, at peace as if he had almost passed. The paramedics arrived and were the coolest looking hipster dudes. It felt like a movie, almost a heist. They didn't appear to be medically professional but we felt safe with them. One of them had modified his shirt to roll the sleeves up and fan the collar out. The other dude had a curlicue mustache. I felt like we were in an ambulance with Mumford and Sons. Aside from our rockabilly ambulance ride, it was surreal. My fiancé had just had a pulmonary embolism and almost died right in front of me. I kept thinking, *I hope he doesn't die because I don't want our last conversation to be a fight about wedding tasks.* I was laden with guilt for a while after this incident. We got to the hospital and met with the doctors. They decided to put an IVC filter into his inferior vena cava to prevent any more bleeding. He had been diagnosed with a blood clot two months prior and had been under doctor's care weekly since. He was put on a series of blood thinners but had two allergic reactions to different medicines. I went home that night at two in the morning, collapsed on the bathroom floor and sobbed while our dog Cleo licked the tears off my face. She didn't understand why her dad didn't come home with me that night. I was unsure if he would ever be back. It was confusing and scary but it was important to remain positive and charge on. Four hours later, at six in the morning, my fiance called me. He was petrified. He had coughed up more blood, this time in a cup by his bedside. He pressed the nurse button and no one had come to help him for a while due to the shift change. He was worried they were not caring for him properly. I packed a bag and headed back to the hospital. Thankfully, I showered a couple hours before I went to bed so I was able to spring out of the house quickly. The hospital ended up doing a great job. This was just a timing issue where he happened to have an incident at the very moment shifts were changing and the new crew was being briefed. After that, we grew into understanding the hospital experience, timing and how to give feedback and advocate for him when needed. There were and still are many days like this where something medically happens, and everything stops and needs to be tended too. Things have never really "calmed down" since that day at the hospital. There are still many emergency room visits, pop up medical events, and hypervigilance with my now husband's health. This has become the fabric of our lives.

He was in the hospital for a week. At this point, we were a week away from getting married, my fiancé almost died, we were unsure how long he'd need to be in the hospital and we didn't know if he'd make it out in time for the wedding. We discussed getting married in the courtyard of the hospital and then I would go to the wedding to have the party since we paid for it and everyone was coming into town. Every day I would wake up, work out, shower, and bring my laptop to the hospital. I would sit next to him as he finally got to watch his World Cup soccer while I worked. I shared some of the situation with clients, but not all of them. Up until this point in my career I had kept a thin veil between work-Mandi and real-Mandi. I was always authentic with my customers but had never shared too many personal things with clients. This incident changed everything. It changed many things about me, my now-husband, our relationship, and our lives. From a professional standpoint it forced me to change the entire outlook on my business. The hospital was busy with pulmonary specialists, vascular doctors, nutritionists, phlebotomists, nurses, and interruptions. There were also many, many moments of deep thought, a deep need to focus, take notes and record detailed medical information being shared with us. This is now a chronic illness that requires daily care and medication. Our life had been pretty carefree leading up to this and now we had to follow a daily regimen and live with the restrictions of someone who needs to be on blood thinners for the rest of his life. This meant no more bike rides, snowboarding, careless hops over the fire, or spontaneous things that could cause a bleed out. Just like that—without warning—our life had changed. Since there was so much action in the hospital room I didn't really have a steady workflow. Because I run my own business, it's not like I could have asked my "office mate" to take on my responsibilities when I was talking to the doctor about my fiancé's care. It was nuts. I was in and out of work emails and conference calls, in between managing communication with family and friends and calming my fiancé's nerves.

This is when I learned to get a lot done in a small period of time. I knew I'd have only an hour—at most—of uninterrupted time a day. I learned to prioritize revenue-producing tasks over non-revenue-producing tasks. The way I manage my emails changed. I started each day with a to-do list. I'd search for the names of the people I was working with on pending contracts in my emails and tackle all of those first. Once I was done with all the top-dollar tasks, I chipped away at the lower dollar ones. I let fire drills and crises solve themselves when normally those would be the first ones I'd solve. After all that was done, I'd pick through the emails one by one. I learned to fire clients that weren't understanding of what was happening to me personally. I learned to put friends and family into the outer rings of my sphere if they gobbled up brain space that I didn't have at that moment. I learned to not let much bother me if it was not moving my life forward. And, I learned to continue to have a positive attitude—about everything. Even on the most difficult days of watching my husband cough blood into a hospital cup as we measured to see if it was less than the day before, I stayed positive. When people are annoyed at my positivity or can't stand me for being upbeat, I don't care. Those people can kiss my ass. I watched my husband nearly die in front of me, managed my business, maintained a healthy attitude and got married a couple weeks later. Something about my positive attitude got me through it and I am loyal as all hell to that mindset.

On the day of our wedding venue walk-through, my fiancé was discharged from the hospital and he insisted on joining me. I will never forget driving around the corner to pick him up in front of the hospital. Our appointment was at one that afternoon and he was discharged at a quarter to one. He was standing there, holding a pillow—in a daze as if he was a baby with a stuffed animal—wearing so many plastic hospital wristbands, squinting at me as the sun beat down on his face. He had been cooped up in a hospital for so long that daylight was difficult and re-entry into the outside world was a challenge. He wouldn't take that bracelet off and wore it all day. I insisted he didn't have to come with me but he insisted he did. I walked around the venue with our wedding vendors, while he sat on a stoop staring into the ocean, breathing the fresh air. I looked back at him a couple of times and noticed him taking it all in. He was thankful to be alive. He was thankful to be getting married. I was thankful for that moment. We drove home. Cleo the Akita pup reunited with her dad and I gave her dad his blood thinner shots in his stomach, got him some water, and went back to work while he slept. I would work while he napped over the next couple of days and was learning how to cram eight hours of work into a finite period of time.

We got married and it was awesome. The normal stress of a wedding day with worrying about the flowers and caterer that would bother a normal wedding couple were insignificant on that day. I was just happy he was standing there, in front of me, alive, and that we weren't in the courtyard of the hospital. We cancelled the honeymoon because he couldn't fly so I ended up with extra time I didn't realize I had. I had assumed this would be a great time to catch up on work loose ends. Unbeknownst to me, the extra time I had for the next six months would be gobbled up by phone calls to medical providers and insurance companies. I would bounce back and forth between triple checking their work, getting revised bills and fighting to not pay for what we believe should have been covered. This was the second wave of prioritization and I had a system. As soon as I woke up, I would tackle any top-revenue-producing accounts for the day. I only did five of the most important ones per day. Once I accomplished those, I had ninety minutes per day to deal with medical and insurance stuff. I scheduled my lunches, breaks, workouts, medical fights, and work. At the end of each day I felt like I had been to war. This is when I learned the value of scheduling all phone calls. When someone would tell me they wanted to talk, I would tell them, "Excellent, I am available on these two dates between these two blocks of time. Find a time that works best for you and I'll send you a calendar appointment." I was prepared for every phone call because I knew that would make the call fast and productive. In the old days, when he would have a doctor's appointment in the middle of the day, I would always go back to work after. Now, I am wise enough to know that it's never just a doctor's appointment. Following the appointment is a run to the pharmacist, or possibly a lab test, or possibly another pop-up specialist visit where we're waiting in a lobby somewhere for hours. I now manage myself and my client's expectations if there is a day where there is an appointment. I tell people, "I plan to be back in my office by two that afternoon, however, my husband has a doctor's appointment at noon. Sometimes I can escape by two, and other times it's an all-day affair. Whatever we don't get to today, we will work on tomorrow." People, in general, are very understanding of this. And, for some people it's brought me closer to them and they've opened up about their life struggles too. Prior to this I never made a habit of sharing anything like this with clients, but I was wearing this like a hat all day, every day and there was no way I couldn't explain what was happening.

Eventually, all the medical bills were paid and my husband and I slipped into a normal routine again. He still lives with his chronic illness but overall is very healthy and happy. Although this was an absolutely awful thing to have happened, it helped me prioritize in a way that has changed me for the better. Now, I am not saying you should go out and have a life-changing event to learn how to prioritize. I am saying, be proactive and look at your day. Look at how you can make the most of the small amount of time you have. How can you cram eight hours of work into one hour and still run a successful business? And once you look at that eight-hour work day, are you really being productive that entire time? What can you eliminate from your day that doesn't move your life or your business forward? Who can you eliminate from your world that doesn't bring your life or your business forward? You have the choice to do this. At that time, I didn't have a choice. I did this out of survival.

The biggest lesson for me during this time was that I didn't have time to deal with the crap. I didn't let people or circumstances rent space in my brain if they weren't paying top dollar. If I lost a piece of business, I didn't waste time beating myself up, I asked myself what I learned, what I could do better next time, and moved on quickly. If a friend didn't invite me somewhere, I didn't ruminate on why, I assumed they didn't want me there, and I was fine with that. I didn't want to be somewhere I wasn't wanted anyway and I didn't waste time thinking about it. People outright flaked on my wedding or cancelled the day before for various reasons. This would normally ruin or end a friendship. Instead of sitting in anger or sadness about the missing guests, I let it go. It was that simple and not worth the time or space in my brain. I no longer spend time complaining. I only look for the good in all circumstances, seek out joy and celebrate the time I do have with people, clients and circumstances. I no longer react to every email, phone call, or voicemail. There are some situations that must resolve themselves. Sure, you can probably resolve it faster and better but sometimes if you give it just a little time, the situations work themselves out. When you give other people the chance to take care of things, it's a leadership moment for your employees, or an aha moment for your clients. And when you realize that some people are intolerant, on the rare occasion that you didn't get back to them in ten minutes because you were taking notes at a doctor's appointment with your husband, then you fire those people. They are not good clients and not good people in your sphere. You will resent working with them if you keep them.

PINK FLAGS: HOW BEING DIAGNOSED WITH SEVERE ANXIETY DISORDER CHANGED MY BUSINESS STRATEGY FOR THE BETTER

Our body and brain give us many warnings before an actual crisis happens, but sometimes we are just not tuned into it. We all know what a red flag is, right? It's that moment when life comes to a screeching halt and your body and/or brain says, "Hell No." This may be with a person, a job, a love interest, or even a co-worker. Many moments can produce that illuminated red flag. *Did you know that you can prevent the red flag by paying attention to the pink flags?* Red flags cause fire drills. Fire drills are a waste of time. On occasion, you're undoubtedly going to have something pop up that you can't prevent. Think about the last time you had a fire drill in your life and your business. Go ahead, ponder it… I'll wait. Did it take up your whole day physically and then suck the life out of you emotionally? Regaining your footing after an unnecessary red flag or fire drill is time consuming and not necessary. So pay attention to the pink flags.

My red flag was being diagnosed with severe anxiety disorder. My pink flags were a series of events that had occurred for years that I just plain ignored. I was running errands on a sunny Saturday afternoon. I was driving with the windows down, wind whipping through my hair, Fergie and I were doing a duet and my car was the stage. I was happy, at peace, and relaxed. When the light turned green, as I drove up the hill, my body started a series of sensations that were very frightening. My ears started ringing. I had a pounding headache. I was dizzy, had chills, and a tingling sensation waved across the left side of my head that went from my eye, to my forehead, to my scalp, to the nape of my neck and back. These sensations repeated several times while I was driving up the hill. I thought I was having a stroke. I pulled my car over to the side of the road. I turned the music off. I said to myself, "You are fine, you can do this." The physical sensations passed within five minutes and my body felt normal again. I went back to normal life as if nothing had happened. I would continue to scary episodes like this for several years before I identified that these were the preemptive strike of an anxiety attack. I ignored the symptoms because I thought I was being "weak" and that I should just "toughen up." I didn't have time to deal with this. In reality, my body was giving me warning signals that it needed to be reset. At that time, I was ignorant to anxiety disorder. If you would have asked me then, I would have said, "It's all in your head. The mind is stronger than the body. Just calm down." This was a very uninformed mindset. Years later, after a ton of medical education, doctors, hiring an anxiety therapist, and understanding this disorder, I cringe when people say things like *just calm down, take a breath, think about something else*. I cringe because anxiety is not something your body can easily control. Some of the symptoms can be amplified by fear of it being a heart attack, but for me, my anxiety disorder is a physical, uncontrollable condition. When your body wants to have an anxiety attack it can happen when you are relaxing in your yard painting, when you're in yoga class, or even on a Friday mall date with your spouse at Bed, Bath & Beyond. Anxiety does not care how relaxed or amped up you are. It does what it wants to do and you have to surrender to it in that moment, or you're toast. If you try to control it, you lose. If you ignore it because you don't have time for it, it will get you in a bigger, more time-sucking way in the future.

The final pink flag with my friend anxiety was one Friday afternoon. It was another sunny, breezy day. I was having a fun conversation with a business associate on the phone. We were wrapping up the call and all of a sudden, my ears started ringing, there was tingling in my arms as if they had fallen asleep, a pounding headache kicked in, and my jaw had locked. I couldn't speak. It was locked in a place where my mouth was half-way open. I awkwardly made the noise, "I'll call you back." It sounded like I was half underwater, or had a plastic easter egg in my mouth. I hung up the phone. I went to my yard and laid on the grass looking up at the clouds while these physical symptoms just raced through my body. They took turns rotating as if to say, "my turn, my turn." I let it roll over me for about an hour. My husband came home to find me lying on my back in the yard, with my mouth open, awake and alert but unable to speak, staring at the sky. He assumed I was doing some sort of meditation and he laid next to me on the ground. He approached me like a golden retriever approaches their pack mates, "Hi hun bun, happy Friday, how are you, you look so relaxed, this is fun, what are we doing?" His rapid fire, happy, panting, drooling questions were not met with an answer. I turned my head to the side, rolled over to hug him and buried my head in his chest and started sobbing. My mouth was so dry and I was exhausted. My body felt like it had been in a bar fight. I said, "I don't know what's happening with my body, but this isn't normal and I am scared." He took me inside and put me to bed to sleep it off. I couldn't fall asleep and my vision started getting very blurry. We decided to go to the emergency room. The ER did all the tests... the EKG, blood, urine, etc. They said, "You probably had an anxiety attack." I didn't believe them because the symptoms were so physical, and I was super calm having a fun conversation with a business associate when the symptoms came on. Nothing was revving me up, the diagnosis—from what little I knew about anxiety at that time—didn't make sense. I went to see my primary care doctor the following week. She prescribed me Xanax and told me to take a half a pill when I start feeling my arms tingle so I can catch it at the beginning. I didn't like Xanax because it instantly made me fall asleep. The anxiety had become so frequent that when I had physical symptoms during the work day, I was impaired. I had to take that Xanax and lie down for two hours until the symptoms wore off and the Xanax kicked in. I couldn't function on Xanax so I was losing hours in my work day. My work was suffering and I was having shorter and shorter days just to deal with the disorder. When an attack started, I had to stop everything I was doing at that moment and surrender to it. It was debilitating for about six months. It interrupted everything in my life. This was not good for business.

If I had listened to the many years of pink flags it would have saved me time many years later. This was truly a circumstance where short-term pain does equal long-term gain. I decided I had enough of the constant and daily interruptions and I found a local expert who specialized in women with anxiety disorder. I met Dr. Wall and she changed my life. She insisted that I have my primary care doctor order me the lady tests that would show my hormone levels just in case some of my symptoms were from perimenopause. Sure as shit, I was in perimenopause. Apparently, my body was having an internal fight between perimenopause and anxiety. The body chemicals for both were jockeying for attention. They were throwing out words like cortisol, adrenaline, and hormones. My body chemistry was out of whack and apparently, I have had anxiety disorder my whole life but it was latent. It wasn't until my body went into perimenopause that the anxiety chemicals kicked into gear, which was why it was so severe. After hearing this I thought back to so many times where my anxiety got the best of me and I wasted so much time getting angry about nothing. I was blindly revved up about many circumstances that were beyond my control and I spent a lot of time explaining why everyone else was wrong. There were many co-workers I was impatient with, boyfriends that I annoyed and customer service reps that didn't stand a chance with me on the phone if I was mid-attack. Something really important I learned about the depths of anxiety disorder is that if you ignore the pink flags (a.k.a. symptoms), it doesn't go away. It keeps going and finds different pathways. Eventually, it manifests past the physical, past the worry, and ends in anger. Unmanaged anxiety can last weeks, months or years and it can sit in that anger phase until you reset your body. It takes over your gentle mind and causes you to have sudden outbursts and be mean. I don't let it get that far anymore because I catch it early. However, this is my official public apology to any co-worker, ex-boyfriend, or customer service person to which I was a royal asshole. When we know more, we do better and I am so sorry for being a jerkface. I had a disorder I didn't know I had—I didn't know how to manage it at that time and I let it get the best of me.

I invested several hours a week of time I didn't have because of all those lost hours of work and embarked on an intense anxiety management program with Dr. Wall. She taught me all about my body, the pink flags, how to stop the chemicals from racing and escalating, and what things I can do physically to slow it down or prevent it. I felt like I got a crash course in body chemistry. I felt so strong and still do. I've learned to not let it take over my day, and to manage my time effectively through the disorder. For example, when I travel for work, I tend to have an anxiety attack within a couple days of returning. Now, I plan for it. That way I am not disrupting my meetings and appointments. When I schedule time to be healthy and to be ill, it actually helps me better manage my disorder. This is the long way of telling you to pay attention to your pink flags. If I would have paid attention to my anxiety disorder symptoms sooner, I would have had a lot less interruptions along the way and saved so much time. Listen to yourself.

Listen to your body. Your body knows you and is speaking to you all the time.

TIME-SUCKING CLIENTS

It took me a while to determine the value of firing a client but once I did, I was liberated. I had this client for many years, let's call him Steven. His business represented 12% of my portfolio of accounts. However, the physical, emotional and time toil Steven brought to the table was awful. When we first started working together I thought something was off. Steven couldn't remember anything, and everything that was needed was a rush job. I fancy myself a great client manager, one that can roll with the punches and adapt to all personalities. I couldn't quite pin down what was happening but it was not normal or sane. Hotels would call me to complain about Steven. I had to translate his requests from "Steven Speak" to a real request so the hotel understood. The hotels and I were consistently fixing Steven's planning mistakes. He was not good at managing time and would do many things at once. We'd be on the phone discussing contract terms, which requires 100% focus, and he would be talking to other people, and be on email at the same time. I would suggest we talk later and that was met with, "No, just hold on a minute." At first I would hold and be captive, waiting for a return. Sometimes he never returned. Eventually, when Steven asked me to hold, I would say "sure" and I would just hang up, blaming it on a bad connection. I knew he would call back when I was needed.

My phone rang one Friday night at eleven (which was past two in the morning in his time zone). I did not pick up. I looked at my texts and I had several from him asking for clarification on a contract that wasn't due for two weeks. My husband rolled over and grumbled, "You have to fire Steven." I waited until the morning to respond and we worked it out on Monday. I asked him if it was urgent and he said, "No, but I was thinking about it so I thought I'd call to talk it through." He was thinking about a hotel contract at two in the morning and thought it would be cool to call me that late too?

Another time, while traveling to preview a hotel, Steven lost a company laptop. (Of course, this was frightening. No one wants to lose their laptop, especially one with private proprietary company information. However, I wondered why this was my responsibility.) I was sleeping in my hotel room when he called my cell phone. I didn't hear it so he called the hotel phone which was so loud it startled me awake. Steven was on the other line panicking, "I think I lost my laptop or left it at the front desk. Can you go look for it for me?" I asked if security had been called and if he first attempted to go to the front desk. He said, "No, because I was in bed and almost sleeping, and didn't want to get up." I said, "Well, I was sleeping when you called. Hold on, let me check with security." I called security, connected them with Steven, the laptop was in lost and found, and everything was fine. He called me back a couple minutes later, slurring, and frantically wanted to talk about what a tragedy it would have been if the laptop went missing because of the important information that was on it and that he would be fired if it was missing. I said, "I am glad it was in lost and found." I hung up and saw him the next day for our meetings.

What's wrong here? I experienced several calls like that over the years with the same DNA—frantic, urgent, needing something immediately for fear of being fired.

Then there were the threats that I would be fired if I didn't do what he needed—which was well beyond the scope of my services. When I explained that there would be a charge for what was expected, he threatened to fire me, again. I referenced previous emails noting the service inclusions and he disputed it.

Between the drunken phone calls, Steven's paranoia about losing his job, his threats of firing me and the general lack of focus and disrespect for my time, I had enough. I silently fired him. I knew if he didn't get my very valuable services for free or close to it, he wouldn't use me. So I gave him a proposal three times the cost it would be to use me. To protect the relationships I had built with the other departments, I set up phone calls with each person and explained why I was over pricing myself and choosing not to work with Steven anymore. Each department agreed to continue to use me, citing their own grievances about Steven. I had thought he was beloved in the company and had not realized this was his M.O. and everyone was a little tired of him.

A couple years later the company approached me to work with them again but with a different contact. I love my new "Steven" and it's been smooth sailing ever since. Although firing Steven was a big hit to my personal bank account, it was the best decision I made for my business. It made space for me to find a new client, and gave me time to dedicate to my existing clients and build deeper relationships with good clients. I didn't realize how much stress that one client had caused me. I didn't realize that every time Steven's name popped up on my phone screen, I felt dread and knots in my stomach. There is no amount of money in the world that is worth that pain and suffering. I waited for so long to fire him because I was worried it would jeopardize the other departments, and the account as a whole. I was worried I wouldn't get another client that would produce the same or more revenue. I was operating out of fear instead of abundance.

A boss of mine told me many years ago that there are some clients that are just not worth the "Dollars to Grief" ratio. **If the grief outweighs the dollars, run for the hills.** Get out. Make space in your day for kind, cool customers that respect your time and appreciate what you do.

sales tale:
WHEN SOMETHING DOESN'T FEEL RIGHT, MOVE ON

I fired a coaching client several years ago too—and this time it was drug related. I always had an awesome relationship with Kelley. We had a mutual respect and similar leadership philosophies. We had wonderful success in the first part of our working relationship. In the latter part of the contract,

I did notice that things got weird. Our phone calls got longer and longer. Kelley's rants became longer and longer. She ranted about her employees, the weather, the price of products, her marriage, and her general issues of the day. I couldn't tell if she was looking for additional business coaching or a friend.

That is common in the coach-client relationship. Even though it's business, many times, I do serve as an uncertified quasi-therapist. I am fine with that, as owning a business is hard and having a like-minded person to kibitz with is so meaningful. Most entrepreneurs put their heart and soul into their business so when an employee leaves or an investor bails, owners do take it personally, and I understand why. I am always available for my clients and have become close friends with many of them over the years. However, this situation was different. It seemed like Kelley was "on something" when we spoke. I wrote it off because it's none of my business.

Eventually, I was approached by Joe, one of Kelly's employees. Joe was a rising star. I could tell if he stuck with it, his sales potential was amazing. There were two sessions where Joe mentioned concern for Kelley's safety based on things he had seen Kelley doing. He said that other staff witnessed cocaine use, and he was uncomfortable with the overall treatment and experience. I encouraged Joe to talk to Kelley about his concerns and handle it directly. We even role-played the conversation a couple times. I don't think that conversation was had. It put me in a tough position. I had been experiencing my own weird moments with Kelley. At this point our contract had expired, and we were working together on a month-to-month basis. Kelley also had been late in paying me for a couple months and was now on a payment plan. I was concerned with how the finances were being handled because I knew a big chunk of money was being brought in by the sales efforts we had made through the coaching process. There wasn't anything else I could do and it was a natural break. The business had all the systems and tools in place to succeed. If they followed the plan I created, they would be fine.

I fired Kelley. She understood but wanted to keep me on for another month. I explained that was not possible and then an hour-long conversation of mostly gibberish ensued. We hung up amicably, but I still felt weird. I knew it was the right thing to do for my business but I was genuinely concerned about Kelley. I couldn't rat out Joe, because that would be a violation of trust. I couldn't tell Kelley I thought she might have a drug addiction because I didn't ever see it with my own eyes. I was only going on a hunch and intuition. I assumed it would be OK because the business was now set up with a good structure based on what I had provided. Several years later the business folded. I have no idea what happened to Kelley. I had heard through the grapevine there were financial struggles but never inquired about it. This cleared the way for me to do other coaching and speaking engagements. However, it was a tough one for me to handle on the human side. I still wonder if I should have intervened with Kelley's drug addiction and genuinely hope she is ok and doing better.

I encourage everyone to look at their client base. If you have any clients that are similar to the ones above, get out, fire them. You are wasting time with people that do not respect you, your time, your knowledge or your business. They are also wasting their time because they don't want to be helped, or only want to be helped in a specific way that doesn't align with your business growth. Some clients are just never happy. It's always good to look at ways to improve your service to make clients happy—but when you've turned over every stone and done everything you possibly can and they still aren't happy, walk away. Your soul, your time and your pocketbook will thank you.

TIME-SUCKING PEOPLE

Think carefully about your personal circle of friends and family. Are the relationships mutual? What do you bring to the table? What do they? Not from a financial or business perspective, but from an enrichment perspective. Decisions about how you spend your time when you are not working, and who you spend your time with, are just as important as how you manage your time at work. We've all heard of "toxic" people before, and I challenge you to consider "toxic time." Just because you've been friends with someone for a long time, doesn't mean you need to stay friends with that person. Just because you have history with someone doesn't mean they're still good for you now. People grow and change, and if people are growing and changing with you, that's a good thing. If you have surpassed them in your growth and they no longer enrich you, it's ok to pull away. That pull doesn't have to be permanent, it can be temporary until you're on the same page again. Each person serves a purpose in our lives. Depending on what's going on in your life, it's ok to move people from the inner to outer rings of your sphere. I have found that over time, people are constantly moving in and out of my sphere. Instead of resisting it, I embrace it. It's important for me that the people in the inner rings of my sphere are positive, kind, interesting, funny, interested in their own personal growth and have something to offer the world. These things didn't used to matter but I've found that I'm a better human and more of the person I want to be (personally and professionally) when I am conscious of how I spend my time and with whom I spend it. I am not saying go out and fire your family or your friends. I am saying pay attention to how you feel when you leave an encounter with a friend or a family member. If they inspire you, make you feel good, bring joy, make you want to grow and be better, then, do more of that. If you feel sad, confused, negative or angry when you leave a visit with someone, keep them in your sphere, but spend less time with that person. Your sphere can still be big but how much time you spend with those in your sphere is critical to your overall success and happiness.

I recently reconnected with a group of professional executive women whom I adore. One of the women calls us her SWIRL. SWIRL is short for Smart Women I Really Like. It's a badge I wear with pride as being around smart women that I like feels good. We have a weekly email where we brag about a personal or professional win for the week. We are all very encouraging of each other. I also recently participated in a panel of experts in the "clutter" industry. I didn't realize there was such a thing until I started researching spring cleaning. The common message from these clutter experts is to look at spring cleaning in three ways:

Physical—your closet, stuff you need to give away or sell.

Digital—your phone, computer and the management of your photos and storage.

Spiritual/Emotional—the people and circumstances in your life that don't serve you.

I had never looked at spring cleaning in such a way before and I probably will always look at it in this three-step process for the rest of my life. It's good to look at things, circumstances and people you need to let go of at least once a year. Clutter, in all forms, can be its own form of a time-suck and can prevent you from achieving your personal and business goals.

TIME MANAGEMENT TIME HACKS:

- Don't let your email rule you. You rule it. Sort your email by person. Don't respond to email by time.

- Make a list the night before of what you need to accomplish the next day. Limit it to five big things. Tackle the five big things first.

- Focus on revenue-producing activities first.

- Schedule one administrative day or afternoon each week to do all the planning and non-revenue-producing activities (i.e. prospecting lists, billing, scheduling, taxes, payroll, software updates).

- Schedule a reading day or week. Put it in your calendar to stay relevant. (Bill Gates schedules himself a reading week once a year. That's more than most of us can take, but he's pretty successful, so giving yourself a day or even a half day of uninterrupted reading to make your business better is worth it.)

- Take breaks. Give yourself buffer time between calls, trips or presentations to recharge. Even if it's ten minutes. Buffer time in the present saves you time down the road.

- Manage your own and your client's expectations.

- Cut the bullshit out of your day. What are you doing now that you don't need to be doing?

- Fire clients that waste your time, bring you stress, hurt your guts, or don't appreciate you.

- Set your office and desk up physically for speed. Try and keep everything within arm's reach so you can grab it quickly for reference. What's within your wingspan?

CHAPTER SIX

the value of value

Understanding your value as a human and your product or service's value in the marketplace is important. Taking action to deliver that value over and over and over again is the key to victory. - Mandi-ism

I cringe when I'm coaching a salesperson or entrepreneur and their first instinct is to drop the price to earn the business. Making the decision to buy (or not buy) is about so much more than price. Yes, price is always a factor, but it's not usually the dealbreaker. We normally don't engage with vendors we can't afford. For instance, we aren't going to spend a day at a Porsche dealership test driving cars, asking questions, and sitting down with the salesperson if we ultimately can't afford the Porsche in the first place. We are coming to buy, and there is value in that purchase. I've found over the years that value is based on what that one individual finds valuable— these are the "buy factors" a.k.a. what is important to me.

What is important to one is not always important to another. Understanding what is valuable to each individual buyer is critical. The last thing you want to do is sell someone on how fast a car goes when they find driving over thirty-five miles per hour to be petrifying. I don't care about fast cars—I am scared of driving fast—so when someone talks to me about horsepower or "cornering like it's on rails," it doesn't register. It's also important as a salesperson that you believe in the value of the product you're selling. If you don't like the product you are selling, quit. We can tell you don't like your car or your software platform or your boss. It's painfully obvious. You have to believe in your product as an inventor, business person or salesperson. Enthusiasm is contagious and if you find this product or service valuable and are excited about it, everyone else will be too.

sales tale:
THE BLIND DATE CONCERT

The first time I really came to understand the difference between value, and perceived value, was when I was twenty-four years old in Dublin, Ireland. In 1999, I won a free trip to Ireland at a dive bar in Cleveland, Ohio. The bar was that great kind of place with wooden tables that gave you splinters in your guts from leaning forward and there were peanut shells all over the floor. I was having so much fun with some gal pals sitting at the table slugging beers. We were approached by a buxom pair of women our age who were wearing skin tight

Miller Genuine Draft t-shirts and fire engine red lipstick. Their hair was perfectly quaffed, finished off by a bottle of Aqua Net. They asked us to fill out a form for a giveaway. As drunk, twenty-four year olds who loved free stuff, we obliged and dutifully completed the forms. Two days later the radio station called and said my friend had won an all-expenses-paid trip to Dublin, Ireland for her and a friend. She took me! It was a trip marketed as *THE BLIND DATE CONCERT: Big Band. Small Venue. Big Mystery.* They flew hundreds of Americans and Europeans to Dublin, Ireland—over Y2K— for this concert. The world was supposed to explode as it approached the year 2000, and I was getting on an airplane for my first trip across the pond.

We arrived in Ireland on December 27, 1999. All over Dublin they marketed the concert with signs: **BIG BAND. SMALL VENUE. BIG MYSTERY.** Every time we got a Miller Genuine Draft beer, the label bore the blind date marketing. They were in a co-sponsorship with another beer company at the time, I think. One of the men from the other beer company lingered around at events with us. He was slightly older than I was, possibly in his thirties. He was average height, stocky with a beefy look about him. He seemed drunk most of the time and was very charming in a Stay-Puft Marshmallow Man type of way. He barreled through the crowds at each event in a jovial, non-threatening manner and we all gave him space, for fear of him toppling on us. We liked to be around him, wondering what he was going to do next. One night, I found myself in the Miller Genuine Draft hospitality suite. There were about twenty of us and the drunken Stay-Puft Marshmallow Man was one of the guests. He held up two magnum bottles of his company's branded beer—one matte black and another matte black wrapped in gold foil—and he swayed back and forth, the bottles seeming very heavy. We were seated as he stood before us to make his drunken bottle presentation. He kept everyone's attention as he swayed and braggadociously slurred:

> **Stay-Puft Man**: Hey, everyone, take a guess at how much each of these bottles are!

> **Suite Guests:** (yelling various numbers) Five pounds, two hundred pounds, thirty pounds!

He swayed a little more with each guess. It felt like the bottles were so heavy they were controlling the cadence of his sway. With each guess, he almost dropped the bottles as he pointed to each person as he said, *"No! Wrong! Guess Again!"*

Finally, he told us and this was a lightbulb moment for me. It was the first time I truly understood VALUE.

> **Stay-Puft Man**: This one is one hundred pounds and this one is fifty pounds.

He raised the bottle with the gold foil as the one hundred pound bottle and said, "We can charge so much more for this bottle because of this gold thing." He pointed to the gold foil band on the bottle and looked at it with wide eyes, as if the gold foil was a little troll that invaded the bottle.

He continued, "It costs the same amount of money to produce both bottles. They are the same. The same damn thing. But, since this has gold on it, people will pay more." He shook his head in dismay. He seemed in disbelief that someone would pay more for the bottle but he seemed proud as well. I couldn't stop staring at him, and both bottles. It was an epiphany I had never thought about before.

So many thoughts were racing through my head. *What if I don't like gold? Would I not want to pay more money? If I liked the black matte bottle more, and it's the same drink in each, then why not buy the cheaper one?* I looked around the room, assuming that everyone else was thinking what I was thinking. However, no one was impressed with him. No one wanted to continue the conversation with him. People winced, looked away, and kept on with their individual conversations. Most people just wanted him to sit down for fear of him falling on them. I was fascinated. I kept asking him questions. I sat there like a kindergarten student in the "share circle" sitting criss-cross style on the ground while looking up at the teacher, wanting more and more information. This was the first time I understood "perceived value." It sent my brain spinning. Why would someone pay more for the exact same thing? Why was this more "valuable" to one and not to others? If the ingredients were the same and the brand was the same, then why pay more? **This is perceived value.** In this circumstance, someone perceives the gold foil band to make the product more valuable and can justify that expense. In "perceived value" if I find the merits of the product to meet or exceed my needs, I will likely pay more for it, right? If you want to charge more for your product then you have to identify the specific needs of your customer and be sure it's meeting/exceeding those needs.

I've never forgotten this lesson. That beefy Irishman holding those two heavy magnums pops into my brain every time I am willing to pay more for something than someone else. It's all about value. Value is determined by what I think is valuable—my needs, my interests. In that circumstance, if you're not into gold foil, you're not going to pay more for that bottle. But, if gold is your jam, I bet you'll pay a little more for that.

The topic of value creeps up in everyday life, all the time. I will pay more for something if it saves me time. To me, time is valuable. I don't have much of it, so if something saves me time, take me straight to the cash register, I'm in. I feel the same about health and wine. There is no price tag in the world too large for health. I believe investing in yourself and your long-term health is worth every penny. And, of course—wine. Wine has made me so happy over the years. I can count so many magical moments splitting a bottle of wine with a friend, family member, great client, or potential suitor—all amazing memories created over a bottle of wine.

The best way to understand what your buyer values is to understand their needs and what makes them tick. Value can be learned at any age. I volunteer to teach entrepreneurship, finance, sales, business and pricing to kids ages eight to eighteen in various schools in San Diego. One day, in a classroom of third graders, we were discussing pricing and value. I asked the kids to take something from their backpack, put it on their desks. I asked them to determine a price for that item and put a sticky note with the price on that item. Then, I asked them to walk around the classroom and look at all the items and think about what they would buy and why? After the eight-year-olds paraded around the room, we discussed. I called on one boy who really wanted to tell me why he thought this one girl's pink shoes were worth his allowance. It was interesting because the other kids were giggling at him. I must admit, the shoes were pretty rad. They were Chuck Taylor-esque, pink, with glitter shoelaces, and they lit up when you walked.

"She priced them at $1 but I would pay $20 for them because they light up," he said.

"What about the shoes lighting up do you like?" I asked.

"Because my mom and dad won't let me have light up shoes," he answered.

To this eight-year-old, it wasn't about the color or the glitter or even the style, he saw the value in them lighting up— because he wasn't allowed to have them. It was forbidden fruit, a novelty to which he had little permitted exposure. The exclusivity of the shoes and the rarity was why he would pay twenty dollars for the low-priced, second hand lady shoes. Value comes in all shapes and sizes and we cannot assume that when we're selling something to someone, it's all about price. Value and perceived value must be factors in the sales cycle.

Those kids taught me a lot about value that day. I sometimes think about this value lesson when I am trying to establish value with my customers. I pay attention to salespeople when they are giving me extra value. Here are some examples of value I've seen or used over the years.

SEND CLIENTS RELEVANT INFORMATION

In 2021, people are worried about the vaccine passport or Covid-19 testing for their meetings. I've sent clients examples of registration links I've seen for conferences I'm attending as examples of what other conference organizers are doing. This costs me nothing. It makes me no money. But, it saves my clients a step in research.

MAKE YOUR CUSTOMERS LOOK GOOD

Share trends and tips. This shows you're thinking about the customer, and helps them stay on the pulse of what's new and exciting. It helps them add value to their position and makes them look good.

BE AVAILABLE AS A GURU OR RESOURCE

I love it when salespeople tell me, "Even if you don't pick me, contact me anytime if you have any questions about the service. Even if it's a question about a competitor. I want to be your resource along the way." This is definitely someone I will call back another time, and I have. This no-hard-feelings approach has won many salespeople a second glance at business for furniture, car sales, and hotels.

What are some things to which you would pay more or something you can't live without? What are some things you can live without yet others find very valuable? When you're pricing and selling to an individual or a company, don't assume it's all about price and don't assume that you and your customer find the same ideas valuable. Try to dig deeper and ask the questions that uncover the needs of your customer. Once you uncover the needs and the reasons for the needs, you will uncover value.

I recently attended an International Women's Day virtual event where three amazing female business owners shared their stories. One jewelry maker really stuck with me. She said she bought an airstream trailer, gutted it, tricked it out, and sold her jewelry out of the trailer to start her business. She traveled the country talking to her customers about their lives, her jewelry, and her art. She learned through that experience that her jewelry meant so much to her customers. The cuff bracelet one woman wore was what she bought after she had her first baby. A necklace someone bought was worn after her divorce and it gave her power every time she wore it. She realized that her jewelry was more than just a piece of metal— each piece had a specific, valuable meaning to each customer. Being new to the business, she did not know how to price her product so she priced it the way she thought she should to make money. After spending that valuable face-to-face time with each customer, she discovered her jewelry was about a moment in each buyer's life, not about a piece of metal. This helped her restructure her merchandising, marketing, and value proposition. Most "things" we buy are really never about the thing itself. It's almost always about a moment, a memory, a motivation. Take the time to dig deep into what that means to your customers and try to understand the true meaning of value in your product and service.

You can't sell on value unless you know some things about your customer. You have to ask questions to uncover buy factors. Asking good questions is an art unto itself. No buyer wants to feel like you're drilling them with questions. There is a pace and cadence to which you ask questions. I hate it when I send out an RFP and a vendor sends me an email with a bunch of questions. The reason I am sending this RFP is for the vendor to make my life better, not create more work for me. I don't mind answering the questions, in fact, I welcome the questions, however, you have to have a little more panache when asking. You don't have to ask all the questions at once. You can ask along the way. You can pay attention and take notes while we're on the phone. Many of your answers will come through just listening.

I actually have a Word document I use with most of my clients that I call The Cheat Sheet. Each time I talk to that person, if a value item is illuminated in our call, I add it to the cheat sheet. Here's an example of this. I was recently on the phone with a client who arrived at a hotel. She was upset that the hotel did not greet her when she arrived for her meeting and that she got a room away from the elevator on a low floor.

This was a new client to me and I did not know these things were important to her. As soon as I hung up the phone and tracked the hotel people down to take action, I updated the cheat sheet: "Likes to be greeted when arriving at the hotel before the first day of meeting, room near elevator, high floor." It took me five seconds to do, but when I can arm my vendors with something that matters to the client, it makes the client feel better and is an added detail that makes me more valuable to my customer. I'm sure many people in my industry are NOT doing this, which gives me an added advantage.

Ask the open-ended questions. It's like a game. I try to extract just a little bit more about each client each time we talk. If the sales cycle is short, and I need to know right away, I'll schedule a call with the intention of "Getting to Know You." That way, the client expects a bunch of questions. If a call is not possible and the sales cycle is short, I give the disclaimer at the beginning of the email, "Hey, I know these questions are annoying, and I want to give you information as quickly as possible, can you ping me back answers to below ASAP so I can get a proposal to you?" That way, I am not blasting them with something they don't expect, and I am empathizing with them that I know this is annoying.

I understand it's not always possible to have the luxury of talking or emailing with the customer. Online sales or even book sales, for example, can be tricky but there are many services out there actually listening to your audience with technology. You can invest in those services to keenly market to customers who need your service. Whenever I create a proposal for a customer I use those buy factors as an anchor. Once you understand the client's needs, put it all together in a cohesive sentence so you're letting the client know you've listened, and you're offering them a solution and showing them what's in it for them, then follow up with an open-ended confirming question.

HERE ARE A COUPLE EXAMPLES:

You had mentioned you needed to save time, so by using me to secure your meetings, I will shave one week off the research process. That means you'll gain fifty hours back in your week to focus on other important projects on your plate. How does this help?

OR

I heard you when you said you're slammed with leads and need to figure out how to organize your business. My custom roadmap will help put all the pieces together to give you a clean and organized plan of attack. You don't have to do anything with it, I will create it, and then we will meet weekly to tackle each task. This way, you can focus on the leads that are waiting for you in your inbox, and don't have to worry about the organization of it, we'll do that together. How does this help get you where you need to be?

OR

When we spoke last, we chatted about how you want to find a hotel that gets your salespeople fired up. How does it help to know that our hotel has hosted ten sales kickoff meetings in the last two years? We have a blueprint for you that excites and electrifies attendees to be amped about sales for the coming year. This way, you don't have to reinvent the wheel. We can further customize the experience and you can know you are working with a hotel that has a proven track record for getting salespeople fired up. What do you think?

These are three different examples using my coaching business, my conference consulting business, and a hotel as the product. However, showing the client that you've listened to them by bringing up a specific detail about a previous interaction, shows them what's in it for them. Following up with an open-ended question not only shows that you're engaged and care, it helps the customer to make a decision. **It shows that working with you or your product or service isn't just about price, it's about an experience you provide. It illustrates your highest level of customer service.**

THE MANY WAYS YOU CAN ESTABLISH VALUE AS AN EMPLOYEE, BUSINESS OWNER OR SALESPERSON

If you want to keep a job, a client, or keep your business open, you must continuously establish value in all realms. You have to do more than just show up, process a transaction or sell a service or widget. I am always looking for ways to provide value to my customers.

My oldest niece is a great example of someone who is working to establish herself as a valuable job candidate in her future career. She is a writer and wants to work for a magazine, online newspaper, or publishing in the entertainment field. Her knowledge in that space is undeniable. She is a hard worker. She would be an asset to anyone that would hire her. My husband suggested she take an economics or entrepreneur class so she understands the business of publishing, entertainment, and media. The business of it has nothing to do with writing but she will be a much more valuable employee if she has something to contribute when discussing readership, sponsorships, advertising, and sales. This woman is so smart and is tackling her future career from all angles. She is learning everything there is to know about radio promotion, online ads, technicalities of writing for online and print media, and podcasts. Since she is not pinning herself into one corner, she will be more marketable. When she finally gets that seat at the table, she will be a well-rounded employee with a voice—not just about her brilliant writing—but about the business of journalism. That, my friends, is how you establish value. Out of the gate she will be ninety percent more effective than most of those applying for a job because she has sought out information that is important to the business as a whole. In your current job, what are you doing to create your own value proposition?

Alina's Tale:

When I met Alina, she did not see the value in using my service for her business. Quite frankly, she didn't see the value in me. Year after year, I followed up, sent the emails, made the calls, and sent the handwritten letters. One day, she was ready, she determined she wanted to hear what I had to say. She was adding people to her team and decided I would be one of those people to help with the growth transition. I am so glad she let me bring that batch of smelly Greek food into her office many years ago. She was first a client, then we became friends. I admire her strength, business savvy, love of health and wellness and her love of travel. We have a lot in common. She's also pretty damn funny and makes it easy to be in her sphere. As a person, she brings value with her knowledge, laugh, and caring demeanor. As a business associate, I value her no-nonsense, candid approach. Here is her recollection of our meeting and our experience.

"I started working with Mandi at a pivotal time for our growing company. The service she provides is INVALUABLE. Her expertise, her negotiating skills

> *& her approach to sourcing vendors has saved me countless hours, year after year. Once I started working with Mandi, I knew she was someone I wanted to keep in my circle and on my side professionally. MORE IMPORTANTLY, I knew she was someone I wanted in my life, personally. Who wouldn't want to be friends with someone that wins dance contests and travels the world?!"*
>
> *Alina Caceres, Senior Vice President Operations, Procede Software.*

In my current roles, I can't get fired. My job is pretty secure—I'm the boss. When I worked on the hotel side in sales or sales leadership roles, I was always looking for ways to be the most valuable, most indispensable person on the team. For example, when I was the youngest person on the team in a hotel I taught myself everything there was to know about the reporting system, Market Vision. Normally, only the systems people were allowed to run reports. I observed that when the sales director wanted a report, we'd have to submit a request to the systems person. The hotel had twenty-five salespeople but only one person running sales reports. We would have to wait for them to get to our request. Many times, these reports were prospecting lists—I am not a fan of waiting on prospecting lists. I want my list and want to get selling. I stayed late every day for two weeks and practiced running reports from Market Vision. I taught myself the technology and the system so I could run my own prospecting lists and not have to wait on anyone to give them to me. Once people on my team realized I could do this for myself, they asked me to do it for them. I gladly did it for them because that meant, as a team, our productivity would speed up and we'd produce more revenue. We were incentivized on individual and team sales. If we had access to prospecting lists, history of events, and market data sooner, we would be faster to sell and that meant more overall bonus money for us. Eventually, the sales director asked me to run all the reports. I know this was way out of my scope, but it gave me job security and it enhanced my skill set as the lowest person on the totem pole. I didn't run those reports forever. I eventually trained one of our admins to do it, but the fact that I did it and knew what a correct finished product looked like made me a better leader too. I could identify good data from bad data and used it as a coaching tool. Running reports was not in my job description, but later in my career as a director, when all I did was read and translate reports, this skill I developed twenty years prior came in handy and I am glad I took the initiative to do it.

How do you establish value with your clients? What client needs do you meet that none of your competitors do? During Covid-19, I cancelled more than one hundred contracts. No one could gather. All meetings were virtual. My conference business was shuttered. I had two choices, I could go to bed and wake up when this was all over, OR, I could find a way to remain relevant, and engaged with clients during the crisis. I chose the latter. I became a student of the crisis. I attended every possible webinar I could on hosting a conference during the pandemic, and with lawyers about contract terms. While attending a live, in-person meeting, I took videos and notes and shared all the data with my clients and hotel partners. I conducted focus groups with my vendors and clients separately every six weeks to share my findings and hear theirs. I shared the data with each group and kept all informed. I wrote and updated blogs on my travels. I interviewed people that attended and hosted meetings. I stayed up to date on each city, state and county gathering guidelines so I knew where it was safe to have a meeting and what protocols were in place. I offered to help people in my industry with their conference problems, for free. My goal was to be so on top of the crisis as it changed, so that when we re-entered the world I was the undeniable first choice when booking a meeting. I worked all of 2020 without a paycheck. I probably worked harder and more hours in 2020 than I have in the previous twenty years in my career. It worked. At the present moment, meetings have come back. Clients are coming out of the woodwork. Clients I have called on for years are calling me back. My value shot through the roof because I remained consistent, up-to-date, honest, funny, and committed. Sometimes to establish value with a customer, you have to demonstrate your commitment. In this case, I had to work a little harder than normal to prove my value but it was worth every moment.

What happens when a competitor comes to town? A great way to crush new competition is to create a value-add for existing customers. If you've been the only hair salon on the block for years, and a new salon comes to town, reward your existing customers for not jumping ship. Give them something—a discount, a complimentary conditioner, a nice new branded brush and tell them it's because they stuck with you instead of going to the new shiny place. A great example of this is my spin studio. The owner hustles like no other owner. Just this past week, I witnessed her establish value with a long term repeat customer and it was glorious. It was one rider's two hundredth ride. After the class, as we stretched, staff came running in with huge balloons and a dessert with a sparkler in it. She asked that we all cheer for him for his two hundredth ride and thank him for the energy he brought to class. We did. He cried. We all got a little teary. The most interesting part of this is that he was moving to Texas. He wasn't even going to be her customer anymore. There was no future benefit for that particular person to her business, but she recognized him anyway. As a fellow rider, I got excited for my two hundredth ride. In fact, I feel like it's coming up soon. Even though he was out the door, she still saw value in him. By recognizing him, she established the value of her business for all of us. Her goal is to build a community where everyone, at all fitness levels feels comfortable showing up and sweating. Part of the thrill of being part of a community is being recognized for your accomplishments. She illustrated that with her balloon and cake show. She showed that she cares about her riders, their consistency and sees them as valuable as the riders see the classes. What service can you add that costs you little to nothing but is of huge value to the customer? How can you recognize your current customers for their repeat business and establish value with them again and again? You must constantly be thinking of ways you can be offering value to your clients.

Another way to add value is to look back at those questions you've asked your customer along the way and see if there is anything you can do to make their life easier. When I get a new customer I like to offer them access to me, anytime. When I work with a new coaching customer I will tell them, "If you have a fleeting thought, idea, or concern, shoot me a text. If I can't get to it right away, I will respond within twenty-four hours. There is no charge for my answer to your fleeting thought or idea. If it requires more than a quick answer, I'll add it to the agenda for our next meeting. If it's quick, I'll answer right away." I welcome my coaching clients to bounce ideas off me, and to use me to prepare for a big presentation, or call. This shows that I am committed to their growth and their business, but I don't always have to charge them for my thoughts. I'll charge them for my prep time and the actual time of the organized meeting, but if it's something quick and getting it off their brain helps them grow and be a better business person, access is free, and that is valuable. I am always looking for ways to establish value with customers.

MORE VALUE ADD NUGGETS:

- If your customer is short on time, offer to do something for them to take it off their plate. Something out of your scope of work that really helps them. Establish the boundary that you can't do this all the time, but can see a need in this moment and are happy to help.

- Share industry knowledge—anything that makes your customer look good or elevates their level of expertise helps increase your value. I share industry articles, stats, pictures, and videos every chance I get. When I see something that reminds me of a customer, I send it to them. Even if it isn't relevant at the moment, I want them to have the tools so they can use it one day.

- Conferences, meetings and webinars—when you go to an event of any sort, create a quick list of your top five takeaways and share them with your current and prospective customers. They like knowing that you're out there, in the field, learning. You also might be sharing something with them they didn't know. Share videos of a keynote you saw, or a quote from a session you've attended. These are all opportunities to give something to your client that no one else is providing. It also deepens the relationship. I always write a summary from every trade show or conference I attend and either text quotes to my clients along the way or send an email to them after. Some people respond, some do not, but I am putting it out there to help further establish myself as an active member of our community and interested in their lives.

Once you can establish value and trust with a client, they will be your clients for life. They will come to you for everything. You become a trusted advisor. During Covid-19 I had many clients that cancelled meetings, and a couple clients continued to have meetings. One client had decided to cancel but in a phone call I asked, "If a destination allows for it, do you want to have the meeting?" The client said yes. I asked the client to make a bucket list of all the places they've always wanted to go but either couldn't afford it or were unable to find availability. In May 2020, it was time to shop for 2021 and 2022 destinations. No one knew what was going to happen with the world and booking meetings had come to a halt. Now I had a customer that wanted to book a future meeting, and if I could find a hotel that was willing to do a deal, everyone would win. The client would be able to book somewhere under market price, the hotel gets business they wouldn't have had otherwise, and I am able to establish some value with the customer. They came back to me the following week with Maui and Monaco for the Grand Prix. I went on a hunt to find a hotel for them in both destinations that was significantly reduced in pricing yet still had availability. I found them an option in each location for 2021 and 2022. The client booked the hotels and as I write this in May 2021, the client leaves this weekend for their trip to Maui. The entire island is almost sold out and they are paying a price that is $500 less per night than anyone else at this time. They bought at the right time. I guided them through the process. They trusted me to know the markets. It's a mutually valuable relationship but only because I was looking for legitimate ways to establish value and I followed through.

CHAPTER SEVEN

seal the deal

Don't be afraid to ask for the business. If you've done your
homework, closing is the easiest part of the sales cycle.
-Mandi-ism

It has been reported that somewhere around sixty-four
percent of salespeople do not ask for the business at the end
of a presentation and fifty-five percent don't even have a plan
to ask for a commitment from the customer. Perhaps it's fear
of rejection or perhaps it's because people forget, but there is
power in simply asking for it. *What did you think? Can I have
your business? What can I do to earn your business? How does this
solve your problem? What hurdles do I need to hop to take this to
the finish line?*

I find closing the deal is the easiest and quickest part of the
sales process if everything else leading into it is done the right
way with creative and strategic preparation. Why would you

go through the entire process we've chatted about in this book and not at least ask the question? If you don't ask, you don't get and I know it sounds cliché but it's the truth. The worst that can happen is the client declines. However, what a gift. If someone says no, that's a chance for you to ask why. Maybe it's something you did wrong that you can do better next time. Maybe it's nothing you did and nothing you can control. Wouldn't it be a relief to learn you did everything you could, it just didn't work out this time? Either way, you win, even if it's a no, it's a chance to improve and grow. Many times the most important part of closing a deal is helping the customer walk through their decision factors. Sometimes they are so dazzled by one factor that it leads them away from the things that were initially (and still are) important. Staying organized and keeping the client focused on their goals during the close is essential. You must remind the client of what they've said is important to them, and how your product/service fits their needs and solves their problem.

Beth's Tale:

Beth is an NBC—a Natural Born Closer. She gets it done. I've seen her interact with clients from the financial, pharmaceutical and medical sectors from C-level to admin teams. Her secret sauce is that she has done all the steps before the close so by the time she gets to asking for the business, she's already won. Her clients love her. They are excited to award her the business. She is equally excited to win but more importantly, her true care and love for her clients makes her excited that she solved their problem. Beth doesn't go away after the deal is done. She sticks around and is available if anything pops up along the way. She is with them for the ride from start to finish. She knows how to set boundaries with her customers so she can continue to focus on selling, but her clients know they can seek sage guidance and wisdom from her before and after the deal is sealed. I have learned so much from watching her interact with customers and co-workers over the years. My biggest takeaway from observing Beth over the years is to really care and get to know your customers and continue that relationship after the close. She showed me that by building and continuing the rapport after the close helps to gain a deeper understanding of the client and their business. She also taught me through her leadership that it's OK to become friends with your clients. We go through so much together during the arc of a sale that saying goodbye at the close can be tough. It doesn't have to be that way. You can remain friends, or stay in touch, and continue the relationship. I am proud to call Beth a mentor, a colleague and mostly, a great friend.

"Closing business is how many sales managers feel their success is measured. Yes, that is partially true.

> *However, the most successful salespeople know that becoming a trusted advisor is the real measure of success! A trusted advisor takes time to guide and help even when it may not correlate to a piece of business at that moment. A trusted advisor realizes this leads to closing business consistently and leads to referrals and closing more business. In my career, I have always admired those that made this their goal and Mandi is one that sets that example for all to emulate."*
>
> *Beth Campion, Director of Sales, Hilton Worldwide Sales*

Follow-up and guiding a client toward a decision go hand in hand. You'd be shocked how many people do an amazing job finding a client, presenting, and making a short list but never follow up. Not following up can lose you a sale. Even if a customer says they won't be ready to buy for six months, you still need to stay in touch with that client over the next six months. Find ways to "knock" on their door and touch base along the way. I love it when I am waiting on a proposal from someone and they check in to say their proposal is coming in a couple days and they just wanted to be sure nothing has changed from the time we last spoke. This is smart. So much changes so quickly and it's very easy to lose control of the sale. A big part of closing is to stay on it and be in control of the process the whole way through. A big part of being in control is through follow up. There are many great ways to follow up with people that don't involve long emails:

- Send a quick video

- Send a quick email

- Send a handwritten note with a small gift

- Give a sample of what's to come by emailing with, "Hey there, I am still gathering information for your proposal but I wanted to let you know some good news about this…" Then share a small sampling of something meaningful so they know you're working on things.

Be sure to track your progress in a CRM, or an excel spreadsheet, or even a pad of paper. Any form of tracking is fine, but be sure you do it so you have a time stamp of the last conversation you've had and when the next action item should happen. So much about the final stage of the deal is about being organized and all the tools above will help you stay organized to the very end.

Once a deal is closed and you've scored a new or existing customer, don't forget to say thank you and celebrate. In our busy lives, we sometimes forget that the client has so many choices. You worked so hard to earn this and to provide a solid solution for the customer. The customer has also put their name and their business reputation on the line by selecting you. Thank them for taking a chance on you. Thank them for the business. Celebrate! A small win, a big win, they are all worthy of celebrations. In this busy life, we are so eager to move onto the next thing, we forget to celebrate. I am guilty of this practice. I have been writing this book since 2017. I was looking for a publisher for five months. As soon as I finished the book, I cruised right into looking for a publisher. As soon as I got a publisher, I started focusing on editing and marketing. One client actually said to me, "What did you do to celebrate finishing writing the book?" I sheepishly and shamefully said "nothing." It wasn't until my mom sent me a gift that I hit the pause button and celebrated. My gal pal Lori, who you'll meet in the next chapter, asked if I could go over to her house for wine to celebrate. I was so focused on the next thing I forgot to celebrate the accomplishments of finishing a book and finding a publisher. Don't do this. Learn from my mistakes. If a customer calls you back, celebrate. If you score an important meeting, celebrate. **If you close a big sale, celebrate. In fact, I recently recommended to a client to create a "Win Grid."** It has non-revenue goals listed on the left side, and the prize she will get for herself on the right side. Once she hits those little wins, she gets a prize. It's a good visual reminder to put energy into all the wins, big and small.

Sealing the deal is important but you'll notice, it's the shortest chapter in the book. If you're taking the time to be creative, be organized, build relationships, and establish value, then all you have to do is ask for the business in the end. If you lose, find out why and apply it to a future win. If you win, don't forget to celebrate and build upon that relationship.

CHAPTER EIGHT

disaster selling

Keeping your head above water in a crisis is what separates
the wimps from the warriors. - Mandi-ism

Over the years I have worked, kept my job, lost business,
thrived, and (barely) survived through various disasters. I was
new to the corporate world and was the youngest person on
the team immediately after 9/11. I should have been fired due
to seniority, but I was not. I found a way to keep my job and
find new ways to bring business in immediately after 9/11.
The Great Recession and Auto Crisis of 2008 through 2010
posed a new set of challenges in a completely different role.
However, I found a way to have deeper conversations with
customers and rise above that situation. Finally, Covid-19
kicked my butt. It kicked all of our butts and at the time
of writing this, is still finding new ways to do so. **We have
two business choices during a disaster selling situation—
deepen relationships so you are ready when things come**

back, or find business that does well during a disaster. Here are stories of both from the last twenty plus years.

SEPTEMBER 11TH

Like most people, I remember exactly what I was doing when I learned about 9/11. I had just moved to San Diego a little over a year earlier. I was in my apartment with my roommate who was from the east coast and we were both getting ready for work. She yelled to me, "Mandi, Oh My God Mandini, look at the TV." This is when we saw an airplane crash into a building. I was disoriented. I didn't know if this was live or a recount of an earlier situation. Our phone started ringing and it was my roommate's mom calling from Massachusetts. Neither one of us knew anyone directly affected, but we were both scared and stunned.

As I drove into work that morning I knew it wasn't going to be a normal day and I had no idea what to expect. I was a catering manager at a hotel directly across from the airport. Being a catering manager meant I was a salesperson for all the events at the hotel—weddings, bar/bat mitzvahs, reunions, corporate meetings, anything that took up event space only. I knew there would not be any events that day and assumed the hotel would have me do something involving the tragedy. When I got to the hotel there were TV's all over the lobby. The AV department had rolled out TV's so people could watch and sit in the lobby. Our hotel had housed many pilots and airline attendants and staff. Since the airport was shut down and all flights were grounded, we had many "stranded" guests in our lobbies. I wandered around the lobby and hotel that day doing whatever was asked. I was a lobby lizard for a bit, which meant I directed people who had questions, and I would commiserate with my team in our offices in between shifts. I talked to guests that were stranded and scared. They couldn't get in touch with their families in New York because cell phone service was dead. They couldn't get on planes to get home to see their families. Since San Diego is so close to military bases, many people were afraid San Diego could be next.

In the days leading out of 9/11, there was a lot of uncertainty about our jobs. We knew the hotel would have to lay people off because our occupancy was low. Many of my friends were being "furloughed" and their jobs were eliminated. I liked San Diego and didn't want to move back to Ohio, so I had to find a way to make this work and keep my job. I started investigating military events. I realized since we were so close to navy and army bases, we had many military people in San Diego. I contacted the MWR offices (Morale, Welfare, and Recreation) for each branch of the military. November was coming up which meant there were many military events for Veterans Day. Since many of the bases had strict search and access guidelines, many events that were on military bases had to be relocated to hotels. I created Marine Corp Ball menus, Navy Officer HS (helicopter squad) menus, military retirement event menus, and relocation wedding menus. We matched prices of the military bases in the area and I attended every possible military event there was so I could network and stay in front of them. It was a success. I accidentally became a military expert and brought many events to the hotel from

October to December that year. I was able to keep my job and some of the banquets and operations people were able to go back to their jobs because we had events. This was not easy. I was hustling. I knew nothing about this sector of business, I was an outsider. Also, I was a very young, and inexperienced, salesperson. I was extremely rough around the edges and got myself into trouble a couple times for not following protocol or being in an area of the base I wasn't supposed to be because I was a civilian. I worked through these hiccups, but there is one hiccup for which I still feel ashamed.

sales tale

SELFISH DISASTER SELLING

In early 2002, I had heard that an aircraft carrier that had been deployed for more than two years was coming home back to San Diego. I convinced my boss to allow me to allocate part of our budget to sponsor a welcome home table at the ship's arrival. My new military contacts allowed me to be at the landing pad with the other military families greeting their families. It took a lot of approvals and permits, but I did it. I wanted them to see my hotel's brand and name when they arrived and I wanted their community to know that we supported them. This way, when they think of doing their wedding, baby shower, or any type of event, we'd be their first call. I made friends with a military wives group and attended their weekly meetings leading up to the ship's arrival. I was so motivated to be a part of the community and show that we should be a hotel they do business with that

I lost complete vision of what was happening. These people had not seen their loved ones for almost two years. Babies were born while they were gone and this was the first time some of them were meeting their child. Spouses gained weight and looked totally different and were feeling very insecure about what their partner would think. Some spouses fell out of love with their partners or in love with someone else while away and they knew they had the hard task of rebuilding or breaking their relationship when back. These military service people were in the Middle East. They were at war. They had seen death, life, and some of the absolute worst experiences they will ever have in their lives. And there I was with my pastries and my Casual Corner suit and cheap pumps, hoping they would remember me and my hotel name to book their event. I muscled my way in there trying to sell my business, and had no empathy or concept of what their reality was. In the meetings leading up to the homecoming, I was pretty aggressive about the placement of our hotel's table. The military wives looked at me like I was crazy. I interpreted that as they just didn't like my tone.

The day came and I arrived early to set up my table with my perfect placement and to erect my well-branded sign. As I looked around, the gravity of the situation hit me. People were standing up straight to greet their families. There were signs, tears, and happy smiles. The huge aircraft carrier pulled in so slowly and hundreds of military service people on the ship stood straight up saluting all of us as the ship rolled in. They stood like statues, saluting and not moving, staring straight ahead stoically as ordered as the boat rolled to the pier. They stood in that position for at least ten minutes. *It's a Beautiful Day* by U2 was playing loudly as the ship docked and I started crying. I was watching all these people reunite with their family. My perfectly placed table was thirty feet from the water. I had a front row seat to the reunions. In the time they were gone, so much had happened in each individual's lives at sea, in the Middle East and back home in San Diego. The world had changed while they were gone. The United States was attacked. Everything was different now. I stood, humbly at my table, not even saying the hotel name, I just gave anyone that came to see me a pastry. My business cards were on the table, but I understood this wasn't a time for me to hand those out. My only role in that moment was to be compassionate and welcoming. I still regret the aggressive stance I took at those military wives meetings leading up to the event, but I quickly got a piece of humble pie that day, and I will never forget that moment. This is the day I learned about having good Business Bedside Manner™. I was able to keep my job because of the pivot, hustle and hard work I put into it. I should have been fired. But, the work didn't stop there. I had to remember and realize everything my clients had been through. I had to continue to learn about the lives of my clients so I could be better for them.

Lori's Tale:

I met Lori at a beach party in 2000. I gave her my pager number. We met for dinner the next night and we've been pals ever since. I've had the honor of watching Lori interact in highly stressful work situations over the last twenty years. She's had death threats, job title changes, leadership advancement, public policy and governmental switches that negatively and positively impact her work and ultimately her livelihood. Through it all, Lori has remained steadfast to her mission. She's remained laser focused on the task at hand and has always, with each experience, risen above to get the job done and help people. Her commitment to helping others to get the healthcare they need even when it's personally risky for her is admirable. With each disaster I've experienced in my career, I call on her wisdom and example of positivity and strength.

"My experiences of "life-ing" with Mandi over the last twenty years have included observing her endless yearn to learn, incredible resiliency, depth of tactile experience and her ability to be innovative in figuring out a way to make anything happen. Above all, her leadership style, while direct, is deeply thoughtful and selfless. At the end of the day, she strives to ensure anyone she develops relationships gets their needs met well above expectations."

Lori Keim, Vice President of Business Development Planned Parenthood of the Pacific Southwest, and gal pal.

BUSINESS BEDSIDE MANNER™

Just like I learned back in 2002 about the value of good bedside manners, every disaster that has happened since has been an opportunity to further define and redevelop that oh-so-important Business Bedside Manner™. If you have not thought about your Business Bedside Manner™, it's time. And if you think you have a decent Business Bedside Manner™, it's probably time to refine it.

---

bedside manner

noun

Definition of bedside manner: the manner that a physician assumes toward patients

- a doctor with a soothing bedside manner
- broadly: a person's manner in dealing with others

The good news for Coelho is that his problem is largely a matter of style, not substance. With a smoother bedside manner, friends and opponents agree, he could probably get the job done.

Have you thought about *your* Business Bedside Manner™ in dealing with others during and after a global disaster? Here are some questions to ask yourself that will help you reflect on your Business Bedside Manner™.

- Are you positive or negative?

- Is your head still in the sand, or do you understand what's happening in the world over the last several months?

- Are you a complainer or a problem solver?

- Do you make people feel good, or do they run for the hills when you call?

- Have you modified your approach to adjust to the changing, swirling times around you?

Covid-19 helped me realize the deep importance of revisiting my Business Bedside Manner™. What does it look like? How can it be better?

There's more at stake for your customers personally and professionally. From March 2020 to June 2021, people were at home adapting to a myriad of elements. Some were homeschooling kids and learning how to divide time between work and personal life. Their creature comforts were ripped away as they adapted to new habits. *Do you know what your customers have been through and/or their new habits?* They've gained weight. They've lost weight and perhaps have a whole new lot in life. Family members and friends have passed away or been hospitalized alone. They're the sole caregiver for an elderly parent, aunt, or spouse. They may have lost their job or may have taken on a slew of new responsibilities just to keep their job. **It's important to take the time to understand exactly where the customer is, right now, and meet them there.**

It's up to the salesperson, entrepreneur, or business owner to ask deeper questions, engage in more conscious listening, and solve bigger problems for customers with kindness and patience. For example, in my conference consulting business, we've gone a full year without many of the usual conferences. My questions used to revolve around dates, rates, and space. Where do they want to go, how much do they want to pay, can the hotel fit their large conference or convention? Now, before we get to that topic, we have to address the deeper issues on the client's mind. More is at stake for them. Liability, health and wellness are bigger issues than ever before. My clients want to know what they can do to make it safe to gather people. What is their company's liability if Covid-19 breaks out at their meeting? What does it look like to leave the house from the perspective of 1000 people coming from all parts of the world? Is the airport safe? Is the airplane safe? Do they provide masks or does the hotel? Whose job is it to keep people physically distanced? How do they have a networking event with social distancing where people are getting loose after a couple glasses of wine? These are just some questions on the mind of the client when considering gathering for a meeting.

None of these questions and answers produce revenue for my business. However, understanding the questions swirling around my client's head and providing expert answers is now my job. Being patient with their questions, having the persistence to pursue expert vendors, and being vigilant with getting the answers will help guide the client to a decision.

When the client decides, that's when I get paid. It's not enough for me to be a conference and hotel expert anymore. I must be an expert in the process of getting people to a conference and gathering people in a healthy, low-risk way. This way, when my clients want to have meetings again, they know they can rely on me for relevant, up-to-date, and reliable data that will help alleviate their concerns. Once we do that, then we can look for a hotel to book for a meeting. Take a minute to think about your business. What is at stake for your customer, right now? Where are they at in their journey? Aside from their "buying needs," what do they need from you? Solving these problems in a patient and persistent way will produce big results for you.

Your customers and their businesses have changed. It's a bit naïve to think that when business rebounds after a disaster, it will come back exactly the same way as it did before. It won't. The volume might return to normal levels eventually but the path to that high volume will look much different. It's important to ask customers, "What has changed for you and your business over the last year? What can I do to make the change easier for you?" Things that were important to your customers pre-pandemic are no longer important. Things that were never a glimmer in your customer's eye are now front and center.

INTENTIONS AND INCLUSION

I'll give you an example. In my coaching business, I have a client who wanted to develop her skills so she could become a C-level executive at her company. She is a dynamo and there was no reason to think she wouldn't be on this path. There were a couple tweaks we needed to make and we set a good plan in motion. As time went on, her views changed and her business changed. Being in that C-level suite wasn't as important as being the changemaker for inclusion. She realized her business was evolving towards an inclusion-based model. She was and always has been the leader in the business in that area. She realized it wasn't as important to be the C-level exec as it was to steer the company in the direction that her customers wanted to go. Before her very eyes, in a matter of months, her customers changed—they evolved. Her business changed. She changed. It was an easy tweak for me to make as we simply redeveloped her leadership strategy. However, I think it was very astute of her to realize the business changes that were happening and instead of hopping on the train, she was planning the routes and leading all the trains on the journey. In what ways have YOU changed since the last disaster? In what ways has your business changed? Have you kept up? Have you made any changes that are for the better? How have your customers changed? Have you asked them lately how the changes have impacted their business? This line of questioning and conscientiousness in your business will enhance your

Business Bedside Manner™ and make your business more productive.

CREATIVELY CONNECTING DURING A RECESSION

It was October 2008 and I will never forget my phone ringing off the hook with cancellations for events. I was working at a hotel in San Diego and handled major corporate accounts in technology, pharmaceuticals, and finance for the West Coast. A major technology company was scheduled to arrive in two weeks for a Global Women's Leadership conference. I was tight with my client and knew how much thought and care she had put into this conference, the speakers, the planning, and the content. She called me to cancel. She told me she had a pit in her stomach. I could hear her voice trembling. The event was so close that we had already ordered food and staffed it. That meant we had to waste food and tell people they would not be working in two weeks. That also meant this was likely the first of many calls like this. It was the beginning of the Great Recession and the Auto Crisis. From October 2008 to March 2009 my phone rang off the hook with people cancelling events. I eventually worked on my response spiel. I knew exactly what to say and how to handle it. It was nuts. There was no sense in "prospecting" for new business during this time because no one had any new business. We had a new president, and we didn't know what was going to happen with the economy. The big banks were crumbling, loans were bursting, people were losing their homes and it was really, really bad. On top of that, if a company did travel anywhere, it was a public relations nightmare. Even if a company was financially healthy, it was unlikely that company would take the risk to gather people for fear of it being in "bad taste" since the rest of the country was in upheaval. I decided to stay in touch with my customers in a different way. Instead of calling people or emailing them to ask them for business that I know they didn't have, I created an email that said so.

Subject line: I don't have any meetings for you, leave me alone

Body of email: I know you're sick of people asking you what meetings you have for them, I know you don't have any. I know you don't know when you'll meet again either. Although I do want to do your meetings in the future, let's hit a pause on that for now and focus on something fun.

1. What was the first concert you ever went to?

2. What's one song you know all the words to?

3. What's one song you belt out in the shower or in the car?

First ten people to answer this email get a prize.

This was an easy email to send because I worked for a music-branded hotel at the time. The email was completely on brand. However, you can do the same thing to stay in touch with your clients when they don't have business for you. You can also find other businesses that do well during this type of a disaster, like I did with the military business during 9/11. In this case, you're providing your client a much needed brain break, and giving them some well-deserved empathy and compassion during an uncertain time. If your clients don't have any business for you right now, find a way to be valuable to them and stay on their radar during a disaster. This is the best way to ensure you are their first call when things return.

COVID-19

Covid-19 was a shit storm for all of us. I cancelled over one hundred and fifty contracts. From March 2020 to November 2020, I worked many hours a week, did not get paid, and was in an unfamiliar space. I was explaining contract terms to my clients and my client's lawyers. No one knew what anything meant, and everyone was scared. Everyone had their own reason to be concerned. On a personal level I was concerned for my own wellbeing. My husband has a chronic illness. We didn't know how Covid-19 would impact respiratory or pulmonary function, both of which are compromised. On a professional level my conference business was crumbling. I had to learn about virtual meetings and the sellable items that go with a virtual meeting. I had to stay up to date on the gathering guidelines for cities, states, counties, and countries for all the places I had current contracts. Those changed quite frequently and I clicked the refresh button on the CDC website quite a bit—those guidelines were changing by the minute. I had clients that thought they could cancel their contract willy-nilly and that they could get out of it. They didn't even think of me. They didn't think of all the hard work I put into contracting their meeting for them and that I only get paid when that meeting happens. They didn't consider or even think about all the free work I was doing for them to get them out of their meeting or move their meeting to a different year. For the most part, clients were kind and appreciative. My godmother passed away during Covid-19. She had been ill with cancer for a long time. We knew it was coming but the thought of her dying alone in a hospital crushed me. It all worked out in the end, but it weighed on me—it still does. We had a ridiculous amount of rain in San Diego for March and April. My backyard flooded. My dog went stir-crazy from not being able to be walked due to the rain. I drank a lot of gin. I was determined not to gain the Covid-15 and was in general worried about all my businesses. Around April, after Aunt Chris had passed, something came over me. I decided I wasn't going to let this run my life. I was going to take control of it all. I would accept there would be good days and bad days. I would accept that the plan is there is no plan. I came to understand that the only thing I can control right now is my mind and my attitude. One Saturday, on a long bike ride, I voice to texted myself the note below:

From April 6, 2020:

"Times are changing and we will pivot. In the old days so many of us used to say "this is just business, it's not personal." For the most part, those of us that made non-emotional business decisions were the most successful. However, Covid-19 has changed all of us, our businesses, our everyday life. EVERYTHING IS PERSONAL. Our livelihoods are impacted. Our time management with kids, spouses, pets, parents is impacted. Our business interactions have been impacted. Everything is personal right now. It's time to look at business a little more personally too. It's time to be more compassionate leaders and empathetic business partners. It's important now, that we care. It's important now, that we think of how this affects others, not just us. The more you care, and consider your customers and business partners, the better you will be able to solve their problems. This is a time to get personal. This is a time to find out how this is causing despair or success. Don't be afraid to ask the questions. The solutions we propose now will be different than any solutions we've ever proposed in the business days of yore. If you are looking at business right now the exact same way you did five months ago, you're old, you're ancient, you're a dinosaur, and you are completely out of touch with what your customers need. You will eventually alienate them and maybe even put yourself out of business.

Nobody wants to do business with that jerk who was price-gouging medical masks and Lysol wipes on eBay. This is one of those times your customers will not forget how you behaved. They will not forget if you asked them, "How are you doing today?" They will not forget that you squeezed them for extra pennies and wasted their time in a lengthy negotiation. They will not forget your price-gouging. The tides will turn. It will be sooner than we think. When that tide turns, we will be embarking on one of the busiest buying opportunities in our lives. What side do you want to be on when the tides turn? I want to be on the side of the first call my customers make when they need something. I want them to want to help me so badly, they can't imagine turning the tides without me. I don't want to be someone they cringe when they use because they "have to" or they don't have another choice. I want them to be celebrating with me that business is back. It's so important, right now, to think—*am I using tactics I've always used? Do they benefit me only? Am I concerned about winning or am I digging my heels in because of principle? Am I doing what's right for all parties involved?* Doing what's right is tough. Sometimes it costs you to do what's right. Sometimes you don't reap the benefits of doing what's right for many years. But, when it happens, you have a customer for life. I am conducting myself in a way where I will be on the right side of this when we bounce back. Are you?"

After this, something clicked, everything changed. I had clients that couldn't travel and go places, and so when it was safe, I went for them. I created a YouTube channel called "Mandi's Excellent Site Inspection Adventures" so the clients that couldn't travel could still see hotels. I consolidated my businesses under one umbrella and created mandigraziano. com. I put my coaching, writing, speaking, and conference consulting all under one roof to make it easier for clients to understand. I created a *journey*. I understood that there was a disparity between clients' understanding of meetings. I did forty-three, ten to twenty second videos of what it was like to leave my house in San Diego, travel to Las Vegas on an airplane, observe a meeting, walk the Vegas strip, see a bunch of hotels and fly home. I had some clients concerned about the airport—I had a video for that. I had some clients concerned about food and beverage—I had a video for that. I attended every possible webinar and virtual meeting I could for as many destinations globally as possible so I was on the pulse of all things conference and meetings. I wanted to be a reliable resource for my clients and wanted them to know that I had relevant information for their meeting so when they started gathering again, I was their secret weapon. I started writing more blog posts for all of my business lines. I started speaking again, and coaching more. The topics were deeply relevant and interesting. I picked up a couple new business and sales coaching clients. Basically, a switch flipped. I went from being worried about my finances, my health, and seeing people in person to thriving through Covid-19 and being a student of the crisis. It felt better to be leading the way than trailing behind. Being immersed in this also helped me have a deeper understanding of my client's issues and be more helpful to them.

Disasters will happen. It's how we handle the disaster in our business that is important. If there is no business to have, what can you do to be informed and relevant so you're the first call when business comes back? If there are businesses to have in another sector, what can you do to find that business? If your industry is dying, what can you do to use your transferable skills to transition to a new industry? I know many people in the hospitality industry left for real estate, or assisted living. What else is out there for you during a time of crisis and disaster, and how are you being its master instead of it being yours?

conclusion

These sales tales I've shared throughout the book have shaped me personally and professionally over the years and I hope to continue chronicling my crazy adventures and impactful stories as they happen. I want to continue finding the humor and lesson in each situation, and remain a student of life and business. I know there will be more disasters and business lessons—I just hope there are no more stalkers.

I also hope that you take a small slice of this book and apply it to your daily life, in whatever way it serves you best. Even if it's just one little nugget or one little moment of kindness or empathy for the salespeople in your life, take it and make it your own. Sales has woven its way into the fabric of my life and I hope a small thread of it winds its way into yours—in a positive and non-cringey way. Remember, we all need sales. It's here to stay. It's time to get comfortable with the Sales Tales in all of our lives.

acknowledgements

Asking for help is not something I do with grace. Writing and publishing this book taught me the value of tapping into my sphere of loved ones and professional colleagues. I am so darn lucky to have so many amazing humans in my life that are smart, sassy, thoughtful, honest and willing to give their authentic opinions, at all costs. Below are just some of the thank you's but please know many are still not listed.

Ashley Bunting and the Merack Publishing family of editors, artists, and strategists.

The Kobasic/Meldrum/Waite/Backo/Graziano families across the globe.

Kathy Kobasic, my mom, the number one salesperson of them all.

My network of gal pals in San Diego, in Ohio and across the country. You are a fierce tribe of spectacular women.

Dr. Alessandra Wall, PHD—The best anxiety/women's leadership coach on the planet. You changed my life. You taught me strategies to manage my mental illness. You brought this book out of me. Thank you.

Danielle Baldwin—The best writing coach out there. Thank you for going "Bruno" on me when I was lagging. Thank you for introducing me to the process, keeping me on task and realizing that my eyebrows raise with happiness when I talk about sales.

Erika Brunke and the I AM REMARKABLE Lady Troop.

The Monthly SWIRL (Smart Women I Really Like) Crew—I stole the SWIRL acronym from Erika.

Past and Current customers of my HPN Global business and Facetime Coaching business.

The HPN Global family.

Sally Viavada, Teresa Marie Howes, Dr Dan Bjerke, Meryl Moss and The Moss Media Team, Scooter my love—again, my best friend and little sis Vikki Meldrum, my big sis Debbie who guided me on which publisher to select, big bro Greg who is the best subtitle brainstormer on the planet, sister Ang who remembers everything and is always rooting for me, bro Brian who crushes in the sales world and his creative genius inspires me all the time, and Captain Dave, my dad, who taught me to always find a way and through determination, I can get anything done.

THE I NEED SALES VIDEO TEAM:

Chad Yarvitz, Ace Viavada, Emma George, Mihir Patel, Lori Torio, Jil Dasher, Donna Lisa Murray, Scooter Graziano, Ashley Bunting, Angela Johnson, Alicia Kobasic. The amazing producer and director of the video Sierrah Nalani.

THE ART TRIBE:

Angela Johnson, Jeremy Backo, Shana Fiducca, Sharon Dallman

THE ESTEEMED PROFESSIONALS THAT PROVIDED QUOTES:

Andy Hottenstein, Shawna Bumpus, Mike Georgopoulos, Julie Dunkle, Lori Keim, Beth Campion, Tim Mulligan, Alina Caceres. I have learned so much from each of you over the years and appreciate you more deeply than you'll ever know.

about the author

Mandi Graziano's long and storied career includes leadership roles in sales and operations positions with major hotel chains, independent hotels and private event venues across the United States. She has been a sales manager, event manager, marketing manager, account director, national sales manager, vice president of global accounts, entrepreneur, public speaker, and coach—all of which have contributed to her growing collection of entertaining and informative sales tales.

Her voice as a customer, buyer, salesperson, and coach are what make the stories of this book unique, with a broad perspective.

Since 2007, she has run her own sales and business coaching company which helps sales teams, business leaders, and entrepreneurs improve their strategies for cultivating prospects, building stronger business relationships, and closing deals. Since 2010, she has been the vice president of global accounts at HPN Global, a global site selection and meeting planning company, where she finds hotels and venues for her clients all over the world, negotiates prices and contracts, and provides consulting on all aspects of managing meetings, conferences, and conventions globally.

Whether Mandi is coaching a sales team or scouting out the perfect location, she approaches every endeavor with her unique blend of boundless energy, expertise, and enthusiasm.